THE DARWEN COUNTY HISTORY SERIES

A History of
SURREY

John Evelyn's terraced garden at Albury, inspired by the Grotto of Posilippo in Naples and such Italian gardens as those of the Villa Lante.

THE DARWEN COUNTY HISTORY SERIES

A History of
SURREY

Peter Brandon

Phillimore

1998

Published by
PHILLIMORE & CO. LTD.
Shopwyke Manor Barn, Chichester, West Sussex

ISBN 1 86077 031 2

Printed and bound in Great Britain by
BUTLER AND TANNER LTD.
London and Frome

Contents

List of Illustrations

Colour Plates

Acknowledgements

My warm thanks go to the staff of the County Record Offices at Guildford and Kingston, especially to Mrs. Shirley Corke, and of the Local Studies Library, Guildford, the Minet Library, Brixton, the London Borough of Merton, and those of Merton College and Christ Church, Oxford. To Robin Skinner, Elizabeth Dawlings and Mrs. Ann Ollis, members of my former Geography Department at the University of North London, I am grateful for much help with the previous edition. I am also pleased to acknowledge the help of Ann Winser who supplied the index for this volume, as she did previously and has helped to clarify expression. Mrs. Mary Day kindly supplied information and I have benefited from help and encouragement from Mrs. Ann Money and Dr. Harry Montgomery. To Noel Osborne, Managing Director of Phillimore, I wish to record my sincere gratitude for his friendly help and advice.

The author is grateful to the following for permission to reproduce illustrations: Agnews, London, 3; Andy Williams, I, XII, XIII, XIV, XV; Bridgeman Art Library, London, XVI, Richard Green, II; Minet Library, 43, 95; Mrs. Ann Money, frontispiece; Dr. Harry Montgomery, 29, 32, 66, 71, 83, 106, 108, 111, 112; the Local History Library, Guildford, 46, 73; Österreichische Nationalbibliothek, Vienna, 55, 57; the Painshill Trust, 62; Roger Wayne, 61; Surrey Archaeological Society, 36, 51, 56, 60, 74; Tate Gallery Publishing Limited, VIII; Trustees of the British Library, 34, 39, 72, VIII; Miss Ann Winser, 26, 85.

Foreword

This second edition of *A History of Surrey*, first published in 1977, has been largely re-written to incorporate historical research carried out in the past 20 years. Of major importance are two volumes with which the Surrey Archaeological Society are associated, the re-appraisal of the archaeology of the county from the Palaeolithic to 1540 in *The Archaeology of Surrey to 1540*, edited by Joanna and D.G. Bird (1987) and John Blair's outstanding study *Early Medieval Surrey: Landholding, church and settlement*, originally a doctoral thesis submitted in 1982 and published in 1991. These two works have clarified to a remarkable degree the early story of Surrey. I have added material from other new sources, notably the two volumes in the Regional History of England published by Longman covering the south east, *The South East to AD 1000* by Peter Drewett, David Rudling and Mark Gardiner (1988) and the companion volume, *The South East from AD 1000* by the present author and Brian Short (1990). Additionally, I have tried to keep abreast of other research papers and monographs, such as Gradidge's *The Surrey House* and those in the journals of *Garden History* and *Southern History*, the latter including some of my work on aspects of Surrey.

1

The Personality of Surrey

Four postes round my bed,
Oak beames overhead,
Old rugges on ye floor,
No Stockbroker could ask for more.
Osbert Lancaster, *Homes Sweet Homes* (1948)

The Search for an English Arcadia

In this book it is proposed to take the county boundary as it stood before 1888 when metropolitan Surrey was removed to form part of the new county of London. For several centuries this historic county of Surrey has borne the dual role of the Londoner's pleasure resort and his much sought-after place of residence. By 1939 the huge predominance of a modern city was found even in the county's remotest corners, for professional and business men have by preference long moved westwards out of London in search of fresh air and a garden. The ever-expanding sprawl and influence of London has now made Surrey the residential appendage of an over-grown monster of a city, the largest the world had ever seen in 1900. The county is now dominated by London as no other county in England is dominated by a mighty city and so there is hardly anywhere in Surrey where one can feel free of London. The gigantic presence and international role of London has been the primary catalyst in Surrey's modern change. Its unplanned sprawling mass wrought a fundamental change of human habitat in Surrey, creating much social and landscape disruption and per-meating the whole county with London's dynamism and lifestyle, so pro-ducing a new mode of human existence, the first and archetypal city of the modern age. So compelling has been the social *cachet* of a Surrey home that the county is much maligned and mocked for its pretensions and character. It is so de-countrified as to have, for a countryside, a too ample covering of asphalt for many people's taste. It now has an urban image, a supposed suburban monotony of housing estates wallowing in lanterned drives, lily ponds, bird baths, clipped macrocarpa, laburnum and rhodo-dendron, falsely bucolic in a manufactured countryside all pretence and artificial, a townee's fantasy of countryside. Nancy Mitford in *The Pursuit of Love* (1945) observed:

> The great difference between Surrey and proper, real country, is that in Surrey, when you see blossom you know there will be no fruit. Think of the Vale of Evesham and then look at all this pointless pink stuff—it gives you a quite different feeling ...

11

This manufactured countryside which is not a workplace but essentially a playground is the key to the essential character of the present face of Surrey and it is due to the reshaping by successive generations striving to achieve ideal forms of beauty in landscaped parks, gardens and arboreta. In the words of Christopher Hussey, the spread of this artistic endeavour turned much of the county into a 'Vast created landscape, natural enough to our eyes, but in reality managed as much for picturesque appearance as for economic returns'. Thus aesthetic landscaping has been as important in the making of the Surrey scene as was the contemporary Enclosure Movement in the East Midlands. In recent years incomers have introduced new forms of landscape. Golf, with its computer-designed cosmetically green lawns and sand pits, has affected the appearance of Surrey to a degree unparalleled anywhere else in England.

The once-loved cosy familiarity of Surrey with memories of blue hills in the distance, glowing fires, cups of tea and buttered toast, now seems to many, over-cultivated, over-manicured, over-contrived and over-built. Parts of Surrey are covered in a hybrid half-country, half-city subtopia that seems almost worse than urban sprawl.

Yet for the one who has mocked there have been a hundred who have enjoyed the Surrey experience. John Betjeman's vision of Surrey was one of unalloyed delight:

> Fling wide the curtains! - that's a Surrey sunset
> Low down the line sings the Addiscombe train,
> Leaded are the windows lozenging the crimson,
> Drained dark the pines in resin-scented rain ...

He found enthralling in the 1950s the train journey from London Bridge or Charing Cross to Croydon, high above the rooftops of South London, and considered there was more to be said for sham half timber than the 'flat mould stuff of the Atomic Age'. Although bits were strung with poles and wires, over-shadowed by factories, offices or ruined army huts, he 'got round to thinking that Surrey was the loveliest county of all'. When he dreamed of the Prime Minister's wife, his friend Mary Wilson, they were looking at Surrey churches together.

1 Robert Skern and Joan, his wife, of Kingston-upon-Thames, d.1437. Skern, habited in a long gown, was 'valiant, faithful, cautious, skilled in law'.

The Perennial Dream of Surrey

Yet despite its urban image nowadays, much still remains of the legendary beauty of the green and lively shire that nourished the hearts of men and women for centuries as an enchanted garden on the accessible edge of the work-a-day world. On account of difficulties with the soils which are discussed more fully in Chapter IV, no wide stretches of waving corn have ever filled the Surrey landscape. Indeed, a considerable part of the county was very scantily peopled until a continuous stream of wealth was pumped in from prosperous metropolitan sources. Surrey's real resources have ever been the freshness of its air, clear veins of pure, hurrying water, varied and ravishing landscape for hunting, riding or walking and the exquisite stillness and illusion of distance from London, always acting as a foil.

The origins of this role of Surrey as an alternative world to London go far back into its history. As early as the 15th century nobles, squires, gentry and wealthy merchants chose residences in the accessible Surrey countryside amidst parks, fields and woods rather than dwell permanently in London.

In the 16th and 17th centuries monarchs and nobles were driven by pestilence, foul air and congestion in London to build homes in country estates in the open spaces in the Thames valley upstream of Kew, and thereafter Surrey has been repeatedly re-shaped by successive generations striving to achieve ideal forms of landscape.

In the Georgian period the conviction spread in both patrician and bourgeois circles that an existence alternately at the worldly centre of London and in the seclusion of a practical rural retreat was the essence of civilised life. This dualistic lifestyle has remained ever since the norm amongst the London élite, though it was not made generally possible until the introduction of railways and the motor car.

It was the coming of the steam engine which led to George Cruikshank's satirisation of the march of bricks and mortar across Surrey nearest to London 'as clerks, tradesmen and even manual workers streamed out of the polluted capital like refugees from some terminal holocaust'. It was the steam engine, too, that created brand new towns in Surrey such as Redhill and 'New' Woking and established colonies of artists, writers, professional and business people within reasonable access of a railway station, so once more re-shaping the Surrey scene.

What the steam engine did not change, the electric train and the motor-car completed. The suburb, the antithesis of the countryside and its enemy, was then gobbling up Middlesex whole and tearing great chunks out of Essex, Kent and Surrey. A vastly expanded white-collar, lower-middle class wanted to exchange dingy, smoky, over-crowded Victorian city centres for semi-detached 'Tudorbethan' homes with gardens and modern conveniences in Surrey.

2 *Waddon railway station in the 1920s.*

Entering unravelled Surrey, the visitor felt transported to an England of two or more centuries earlier with a traditional rural life of its own, and where as late as 1857 people still lived the self-supporting life that William Cobbett had wished to see restored to all. Surrey became recognised as one of the last entrenchments of the traditions and virtues which the successful cherished as most truly English. Surrey thus became an effective remedy for minds deeply injured by noise, congestion, squalor and smoke.

The set of human responses to 'the country way of life' in Surrey has had many guises. It has included the

3 *Cornelius Varley*, A House in West Humble Lane, Norbury, Mickleham *(c.1806). This house was near Fetcham where Dr. Thomas Monro, patron of many young artists, including Girtin, Turner, Linnell and Cotman, had a country cottage where painting sessions were held under the tuition of John Varley.*

very different, if overlapping, practice of a conscious attempt at a simpler existence (The Simple Life), daily commuting between metropolitan villages and the city, weekending, retirement, pleasure-farming, solitary contemplation, country writing, the revival of arts and crafts, and myriad open-air leisure pursuits. These different activities have created their own special forms of habitat. The list is long but includes villadom, suburbia, shack plot-land communities, dormitory villages, model farms, estate villages, bungalow settlements, holiday camps, youth hostels, golf clubhouses, tea shops, petrol filling stations and roadhouses. Golf has also created the special kind of English suburb which imitates the village at St George's Hill and Wentworth.

Yet Surrey is full of paradoxes. Although there has probably never been a time when Surrey was not geographically an extension of London, Surrey has experienced until comparatively recently a distinct rural landscape, a distinct rural society and ways of life. Although on London's border, Surrey was not truly London's countryside until its appalling roads were improved from the mid-18th century. Another reason for the lack of a close contact with London until early modern times is that Surrey agriculture never made a major contribution to the feeding of London.

Before the early 19th century Surrey possessed exceptional diversity within its overall geological framework of hills and vales. This was in consequence of the very gradual evolution of many different local landscapes and economies shaped by people of once rather different backgrounds and folklore and even dialect, and developed at different rates and in different ways. These co-existed as complementary neighbouring districts. It is the very variety of these formerly distinctive little lands and local cultures that constitutes the essence of Old Surrey and is reflected in the local history collections of its numerous museums. Current planning policies are aimed at preserving what is left of this old character. This network of human relationships in Surrey based on the natural diversity of the county was in turn increasingly overlain by the other relationships emanating from London, notably from the late 18th century.

Moreover, despite Surrey's urban image, it is much more rural in reality. Within its comparatively tiny space (for Surrey is one of the smallest of English counties), it has contrived to house just over one million of population outside built-up South London, so making it one of the most densely populated counties of England, and yet it retains a greater variety of rural beauty than anywhere else in so small a space. In part this is because of Surrey's astonishing power of absorption. It has such a happy knack of

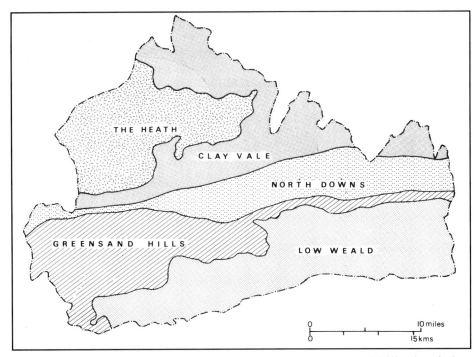

THE HEATH

CLAY VALE

NORTH DOWNS

GREENSAND HILLS

LOW WEALD

0   10 miles
0   15 kms

4 *The Natural Regions of Surrey. These closely correspond to the geological build of the county.*

tucking away big houses from view in folds in its wooded hills that it has been said that only from a helicopter are they made visible.

The Diverse Man-made Landscape

Human influence on the landscape began about ten thousand years ago. Since then men have cleared woodlands, drained marshes and reclaimed heaths. They built houses, shaped fields, wore down trackways. They have sown and reaped a thousand or more crops in fields which we now hold in trust for those who will follow. In so doing they turned a once savage wilderness into a landscape so little like the wild that Surrey has long been regarded as part of the Garden of England.

These activities of man in Surrey have been played out in a landscape which is the joint product of man and nature. Its essence is a remarkable variety of surface. Thinking of Surrey, one recalls to mind not one landscape but a mosaic of four—the still densely wooded Weald; the wild, rough sweeps of heathland around Hindhead and Leith Hill; the Chalk upland of the North Downs; and the quiet, reposeful vales which interweave the other landscapes together. Surrey is rich in strong and unexpected contrasts because its geology is unusually varied over short distances. The key factor in these differences from a farming point of view was the workability of the soils. This ranged from ease of working on sandy loams on which it is not difficult to keep a plough straight, to considerable difficulty on the dry, thin, flinty chalk soils, which caused the plough to jump and every nerve to be strained in keeping a furrow; and the impossibility of ploughing the cold, wet, unkind Wealden clays except in favourable

5 *Helen Allingham's residence at Sandhills, Witley, yielded numerous paintings of cottages and gardens.*

weather. There were also, as will be more fully explained later, important differences in inherent soil fertility. Thus each of the comparatively small contrasting soil regions in Surrey set different conditions for human use. One of the main themes of this history is the play of the economic, social and cultural forces on each of these regions, so producing their differing, and at times, divergent development. In tracing their history we feel the strength of natural forces that shaped people's lives and the human energy with which they shaped their local landscape. At the present time these old differences are reflected in differing building materials such as brickwork around Dorking, stone ashlar at Lingfield and Smallfield Place (regarded as the best example of a stone-built manor house in Surrey) and the golden-coloured Bargate stone of south-west Surrey, together with the half-timbered wattle and daub houses in the Weald.

William Cobbett (1762-1835), whose ability to infer the influence exerted by the sub-soil on surface cultivation has probably never been equalled, has expressed this scenic variety in agricultural terms: 'The county of Surrey presents to the eye of the traveller a greater contrast than any other county in England. It has some of the very best and some of the worst lands, not only in England, but in the world'. In a rare record of his aesthetic contentment he also penned a word picture of the diverse country of the Wey valley between Godalming and Guildford: 'Here are hill and dell in endless variety. Here are Chalk and sand, vying with each other in making beautiful scenes. Here are woods and downs. Here is something of everything but fat marshes and those skeleton-making agues'. It is this upper valley of the Wey, which Cobbett considered the most agreeable and 'happy-looking' he had ever seen, that brings all Surrey together, both the rich alluvial and valley land and the intermingled poorer land on the Chalk and Lower Greensand formations. In many ways this little district between Milford and Guildford is the core and centre of the richly complex world of old Surrey, the county's cradle, so to speak, and a microcosm of the whole. Here we find evidence of relatively dense prehistoric settlement, and of later pagan Saxons worshipping idols in the woodland groves, the first Surrey towns, and a flourishing

medieval cloth industry. Near our own time, its scenery and buildings visibly inspired Gertrude Jekyll to create new styles of garden design and the same corner of Surrey had an important influence upon the career of Edwin Lutyens, the architect.

The Weald Clay supports a luxuriant growth of trees and shrubs, especially oak, but the wood-clearing Saxons who moved in to wrest fields from the forest found it a hard land to win and a hard land to hold. The soils are tenacious and thus difficult to plough in adverse seasons and they

6 *Gertrude Jekyll: a portrait by Sir William Nicholson.*

require large artificial increases in manure. It was the imperious necessity of new land for a growing population which brought into existence raw, unfinished communities in the woodland clearings attached to parent centres in the older settled Vale of Holmesdale and still further north. Unknown families, apparently between the eighth or ninth and 13th centuries, generation by generation, set their hands to the centuries-long task of taming the Surrey Weald and applied the strength and ardour towards a life of increasing comfort and wealth. This winning of new land from the forest was the achievement of small-holding forest dwellers—hard, bold, sturdy, unsophisticated, and as strong as the soil they worked upon. In plying their axes to clear patches of the forest and to fence off a few acres round their rough huts they had to learn new ways of living from those practised on the older settled parts of Surrey developed on more favourable soils, whence they had come. Amongst new skills they acquired were forestry and woodcrafts, for the forest dwellers soon learned that trees were the best crop on the heaviest clays, for bad times and wet seasons did not touch the Surrey woods.

The later history of man's occupation of the Weald is marked by recurrent setbacks. Such periods of adversity are interspersed between more prosperous and stable ones. Examples of 'lean' years are several runs of bad seasons between 1300 and 1480; the recession following the decline of the charcoal iron industry at the end of the 17th century; the dismal 1830s, 1870s and 1930s. Conversely, the 'fat' years of the mid-13th century, the early 1600s and the Napoleonic Wars (1793-1815) are also readily identifiable.

In north-west Surrey the salient feature of the landscape before the early 19th century was the great sand-waste on the sterile soils of the Bagshot formation. This consisted almost entirely of sand covered with heather and fern, and studded with large peat-bottomed meres and marshes on impervious ironstone layers ('hard-pan'). The boggy patches, haunted by myriads of wildfowl, were still called 'moors' by the local folk as late as the last century from a word derived from Old English *mora*, a bog. The reclamation of these heathlands played an important part in the development of a regional peasant society in Surrey. It was by far the worst land in Surrey from which medieval man produced his daily bread. With no deep rich soil at their disposal peasants burned and tore up the broom, gorse and heather to make fields, and dried out marshy hollows. The heath gradually shrank before the efforts of land-hungry peasants in the 13th and early 14th centuries by which time virtually all the better land, including that of the Weald, had previously been brought to agricultural use. Most of this former wild lay within the Royal Forest of Windsor or was held by the great Abbeys of Chertsey and Westminster, both of which had received large grants of the waste. The sterility of the sands made reclamation slow and difficult, and after the heavy mortality of the Black Death in 1348 many enclosures reverted to waste and were not again improved until the 17th century.

Even as late as 1830 large tracts of the sand-waste remaining survived unmastered, 'unscarred by a single human dwelling, scarcely changing from century to century', for the soil was too poor to have tempted reclamation on any large scale. In the 1850s travellers by the Southampton railway were

7 *The road between Shere and Ewhurst. Deeply sunken hollow-ways are distinctive features of the west Surrey sandstone outcrops.*

astonished to find themselves 'whirling through miles of desert' within an hour's travelling distance of London and in sight of only the little holdings of squatter families, locally known as 'broom squires', considered the most primitive form of rural society in Surrey. By the late 19th century the Surrey heaths were coming into the hands of builders. The cheapness and suitability of heathland for building imparted the conviction that 'pine country' within commuting distance of London gave 'real and abiding advantages for modern country life'. The late Victorian middle class perceived 'pine country' as providing the best soil, the purest air and the healthiest surroundings and the 'rush to the pine woods' in the wild corners of Surrey became a minor urban exodus.

On the north of the little vale of the river Wey, which is continued eastwards across Surrey as the Vale of Holmesdale, the North Downs rise suddenly and steeply like a spine. The boldest of these hills—often in the past called 'Chalk-pit Hills' because half the mortar of London and countless loads of lime for Surrey crops was scooped out of their gleaming white hillsides—is White Hill, near Caterham. On these summits was for centuries the sheep walk which brought prosperity in the form of the cloth industry to the towns and villages at their feet. The Vale was formerly the most heavily populated part of Surrey. Its tightly-clustered villages (though they had shrunk before recent modern growth) and fine examples of half-timbered houses are tokens of this former prosperity.

Another belt of land of below average agricultural value was that of the Clay Vale, largely on the London Clay. This heavy land gave rise to some of the poorest farming in the county. On the margin of London its cold, sour soil could be ameliorated with London dung and bonemeal but generally speaking it was kept traditionally as woodland or poor grass which was periodically ploughed to improve the sward or for corn. Such land was tilled with great difficulty until the use of field drains from the 1840s.

2

In the Beginning

Prehistoric Surrey has been sadly neglected in favour of more impressive remains elsewhere but the last twenty years or so have witnessed a revival of interest. The Runnymede site is recognised as one of the most significant Bronze-Age finds in Britain since the War. Yet man's exploitation and impact on the environment of 'Surrey' is still imperfectly known. A fundamental problem in later prehistory is to reconstruct the nature of the changing terrain and to what extent previous human landscapes have been lost through changes in the physical environment resulting from the erosion and deposition of the River Thames and its tributaries and vegetation altered by man. This essential framework for the setting of man's sequence of occupation has still not been worked out. Although our knowledge of the later periods of prehistory are now greatly enlarged, the information still leaves much to be desired.

Hunters

It is possible that man first entered 'Surrey' in a warm phase of climate between glaciations known as the Cromerian interglacial period about 500,000 years ago but no certain evidence of him has yet been found to match the antiquity of 'Boxgrove' Man near Chichester in Sussex. The classic flight of river terraces at Farnham has produced the best known sequence of intermittent hunting groups. The oldest humanly struck flint hand-axes (palaeoliths) are found in the highest terrace (A in fig.10). They are of disputed age but possibly some 400,000 years old, representing human activity after the River Thames had been pushed by glaciation from a former course through the Vale of St Albans to one north of Heathrow Airport. As the river and its tributaries eroded the land it spread sediments on lower terraces. On terraces B and C in fig.10 hand-axes are believed to have come from the long geological period called the Wolstonian existing from c.350,000 to 120,000 years ago and implements on terrace D have been identified by J.J. Wymer with the period known as the Devensian some 70,000-13,000 years ago, when the Wey and Blackwater rivers were diverted into their present valleys.

   Another group of very early Stone-Age (Palaeolithic) sites of man occurs on the high plateaux of the North Downs, e.g. on Walton and Banstead heaths. These may have been of the same age as those on Terrace B at

8 *Palaeolithic flints from Surrey.*

19

9 John Linnell's Contemplation is a 'discovery' of Surrey 'wildscape' which reflects Victorian artists' renewed interest in woodland beauty.

Farnham. There is also a small scatter of palaeoliths on the Thames gravels between Windsor and Battersea, indicating that the flood plain of the river was especially attractive to hunters.

For the greater part of this enormous span of time 'Surrey' culture appears to have been virtually static. Yet significant changes in tool manufacture are apparent at certain periods. The most important of these was that, instead of flaking flint cores into crude hand-axes, scrapers, etc., cores were carefully prepared so that large flakes of pre-determined shape could be struck off for use as multifunctional tools. This 'Levallois' technique has been noted throughout western Europe about 150,000 B.C.

These earliest people in 'Surrey' hunted, fished, and foraged in small groups. Given the finite nature of resources and the need to move when resources became depleted, the population exploiting 'Surrey' many hundreds of thousands of millennia ago might well have comprised only a single band of hunters. Although 'Surrey' never disappeared under ice during cold periods it has to be envisaged as rigorously cold, cheerless and barren as are the Arctic and Sub Arctic tundra at the present day. In warm phases (known as interglacials) tundra vegetation gave way to steppe and, with still rising

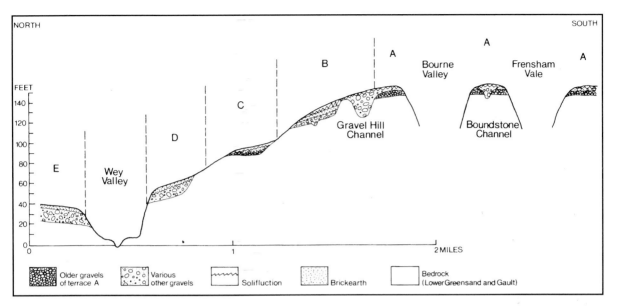

NORTH   SOUTH

10 *Diagrammatic section across the Wey Valley at Farnham to show the sequence of terraces (after Roe 1981).*

temperatures, successively to birch and pine forest and thence to mixed oak forest in the warmest periods before reverting stage by stage in reverse with the onset of the next glacial period. With changes in vegetation came changes in fauna. At the climax of warm periods temperatures were in excess of today's and horse, deer, wild cattle, rhinoceros and elephant were hunted, although most of the human diet would probably have comprised wild plants.

The repeatedly contrasting environment of warm and cold phases, in many ways utterly different from that of the present time, has left a legacy of loess (much redeposited by rivers as brickearth) and chalky mud slides with angular flint boulders which slid on thawed ground in summer over permanently frozen sub-soil and forming spreads of Coombe Rock on the flanks of the North Downs. A remarkable natural phenomenon which is still traceable in the present landscape was the creation of pingos. These resulted from an intrusion of water between frozen soil and the land surface. On melting the resulting hummock collapsed, leaving a crater as at Elstead Bog where pollen preserved from a long succession of trees, shrubs and plants has yielded one of the most valuable vegetation histories for southern England.

As the climate improved after the last glaciation between *c.*18000-11000 B.C. hunters moved back to begin the continuous process of settling Surrey which has remained unbroken to the present. Recent research has established the rapidly changing succession of vegetation to a climax of deciduous woodland in which the Mesolithic hunters lived. These nomads made distinctive hollowed flint points (microliths) generally called 'Horsham' points after the Sussex town where they were first recognised by J.G.D. Clark. The area of south-west Surrey, thanks to work by W.F. Rankine, has yielded more evidence of Mesolithic occupation on the Lower Greensand formation than any other district in south-east England. Its most characteristic legacy is the chipping floor where flint derived from the North Downs was prepared by flaking into flint-points for arrow shafts, knives, saws, gauges and scrapers. The many thousands of such implements collected for this period from Surrey is evidence of intense hunting activity over all kinds of terrain, especially on free-draining sands and gravels, dissected by rivers and pock-marked by meres supporting wildfowl, and better drained parts of the Weald Clay on Paludina limestone patches. It has been noted that most of the hunting occupation on the Lower Greensand is in the first half of the Mesolithic, say to about 6000 B.C. Abandonment of the hunting grounds may have arisen from the destruction of woodland, to attract game, leaving a degraded soil structure changing from a forest brown earth when colonised by trees to a podsolised heath.

Dwellings in summer were probably basically huts or tents, possibly of light timber clothed with turf or bracken, which have left no trace. 'Winter houses' may have been so-called 'pit dwellings', although doubt has arisen as to whether any of these are indeed Mesolithic. The Abinger Manor Farm site excavated by Dr. L.S.B. Leakey and deemed to be the oldest humanly-made dwelling preserved in Britain is now regarded as of later origin and even its use as a dwelling is disputed. The most convincing examples of 'pit dwellings' are in Weston Wood at Albury, where traces of stake holes, with a wider gap as an entrance, were found in shallow pits.

11 *The Mesolithic occupation of Surrey (after W.F. Rankine,* The Mesolithic of South England, *Surrey Archaeological Research Paper no.4 [1956]).*

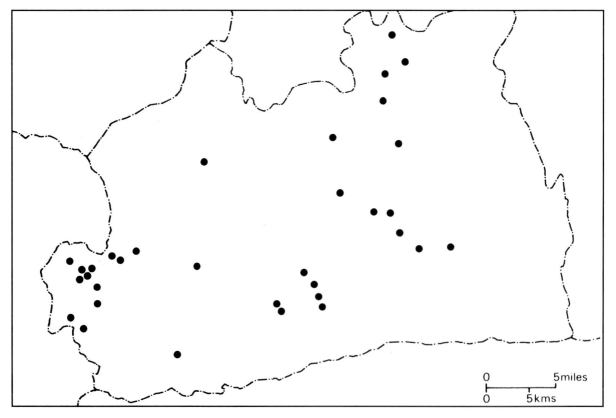

0   5miles

0   5kms

The First Farmers

The onset of the first farmer-herders in the Neolithic period from *c*.4000 B.C. who brought from the continent the inventions of agriculture and the art of pottery, flint-mining and barter or trade is poorly represented in Surrey. In part this would seem to reflect the better environments in Hampshire, Sussex and Kent for light-soiled prehistoric civilisations on the Chalk outcrops. Early farming may have evolved gradually through domestic herding in the Mesolithic hunting economy. Many parts of the North Downs are plastered with Clay-with-Flints, probably supporting a dense cover of oak and beech which would doubtless have required much effort by the heavier iron axes of the Iron Age for its clearance. Not a single flint-mine has been discovered in Surrey, whereas the chalklands of Norfolk, Wiltshire, Berkshire and Sussex were centres of a flourishing mining and farming activity by 4000 B.C.

It is in the Neolithic period that the dual North Downs trackway probably first came into use. This lay in a narrow corridor between the forested Weald and the also heavily wooded Vale of the Thames sloping northwards, and it provided access between the more desirable habitation sites of early men in Wiltshire and those on the channel coast of Kent and Sussex. Known as the Harrow Way in Hampshire and the Pilgrims' Way in Surrey, it forms a continuous trackway at the foot of the Chalk escarpment. This was probably a 'winter' route for the chalky soils were relatively dry. This lower route is duplicated by a ridgeway which would have afforded easier going than the Pilgrims' Way when the heavy mire dried out in summer. Yet another ridgeway is provided by a branch running along the line of the Lower Greensand hills between St Martha's and Seale.

The habitation of Surrey in the ensuing Bronze Age is much clearer than it was 20 years ago. A cluster of sites has recently been discovered in the Thames valley in north-west Surrey of which a well-preserved site at Runnymede Bridge is the most significant. The river bank was carefully revetted with vertical stakes driven into waterlogged land presumably to protect the settlement from floods and to act as a quay for the exchange of goods by river traffic. A dense spread of post holes suggests close-set buildings. A wide range of craft activities took place including weaving, flint-working and metal-working. There is evidence of continental imports including a notch-backed bronze razor and a bare-headed pin together with amber and shale. Pasture farming in the Thames valley appears to have been on a considerable scale and Drewett has suggested that the water meadows on the flood plain might have been managed, because extensive ditch systems are recorded on aerial photographs. A quite different type of major settlement is represented by round enclosures on higher land overlooking the Thames valley at St Ann's Hill, St George's Hill, Caesar's Camp near Wimbledon and Queen Mary's Hospital at Carshalton. Other Bronze-Age settlers are only known to us as builders of barrows on the Lower Greensand hills such as at Godstone, Oxted, Reigate and Puttenham.

12 Butser Ancient Farm: the Round House.

The overall pattern of settlement in Iron-Age Surrey suggests a major shift away from the over-exploited gravels and sands of north-west Surrey but at the same time an avoidance of the Lower Greensand and Weald Clay south of the North Downs. The main concentration of human life appears to have been the valleys of the Thames and its tributaries. The most characteristic monuments are the 'camps'. Some of these have feeble ramparts and were doubtless largely stock compounds. More spectacular are the hill-forts of the late Iron Age when defences were raised against invaders from Northern France. There is an important group of promontory and other hill and plateau forts still conspicuous along the range of Lower Greensand hills at Hascombe, Holmbury and Anstiebury. Dry Hill, Lingfield, deeper into the Weald, has an enclosure of 24 acres and a circumference of nearly a mile. The 'camps' at Farnham and Wimbledon and the ill-fated one at St George's Hill, Weybridge, which contains modern houses within its ramparts, are examples in the Thames valley. None of these hill-forts has been fully investigated and their precise function is still debatable. They are too small to be reckoned as embryonic towns. They were possibly the headquarters of lordships containing many scattered farms. The Wealden forts are the first signs of a permanent, settled economy based on the forest which would have become of crucial importance by reason of its iron deposits.

Iron-Age farms have been identified at West Clandon and Hawks Hill, Leatherhead, and an ever-increasing list now suggests that a chain of them covered the Downs free of Clay-with-Flints. At Leatherhead the farmstead is of the Little Woodbury type. The main dwellings would have been a large round house and the pits and post holes have been orthodoxly interpreted as grain storage pits, raised granaries and corn drying racks. Few good examples of the familiar patchworks of small, squarish 'Celtic' fields have been traced in Surrey; the system on Farthing Down, Coulsdon, not discovered until 1945, is the best known.

The explanations of the maze of pits, post-holes, ditches, banks, pottery and bones found and minutely recorded on Iron-Age farm sites are being tested at the Butser Ancient Farm Research Project, just across the Surrey-Hampshire border now at Chalton, near Petersfield, the first attempt in Britain to reconstruct an Iron-Age farm and work it as it might have been in *c*.300 B.C. The visitor sees thatched round-houses, small rectangular fields sown with Emmer and Spelt wheat and Celtic beans, with other primitive species of domesticated plants. A flock of diminutive, dark-woolled Soay sheep in wattle-herded enclosures, Dexter cattle (reminiscent of the leggy Iron-Age *Bos longifrons*) and pigs bred from the first cross of a wild boar and a Tamworth sow, were selected as the nearest living descendants to prehistoric domestic animals. Experiments are being conducted to throw light on the daily economy of small Iron-Age farmsteads. These include studies of the yields of crops sown in fields cultivated by a light plough of prehistoric type and drawn by an ox team. Altogether the project founded and still led by Dr. Peter Reynolds has revealed a much more sophisticated, efficient and productive economy than was formerly realised.

Romano-Britons

Roman Surrey has recently been re-assessed by D.G. Bird. Most of 'Surrey' during the Roman occupation was divided between the neighbouring tribal territories of the Cantiaci, whose capital was at Canterbury, and that of the Atrebates governed from *Calleva Atrebatum* (Silchester). The most important development affecting 'Surrey' was the founding of London itself as a great centre of communication by land and sea with a large population providing an important market for food and consumer goods. We have a general picture of a well-organised villa life at Ashtead and Rapsley; of a string of London outposts such as Ewell which began as posting stages on the new roads and of important pottery and tile works, probably largely dependent upon the London market. The part of 'Surrey' nearest London probably assumed the special character of the hinterland of a major city. Opportunities for further excavation are taken by archaeologists as they occur, which are unfortunately few. One of the most serious gaps is the lack of information about many aspects of the villas, particularly their economy and settlement patterns. In the heavily built-up parts of Surrey there are still major questions remaining (fig.13).

13 *Roman Surrey (after the Ordnance Survey).*

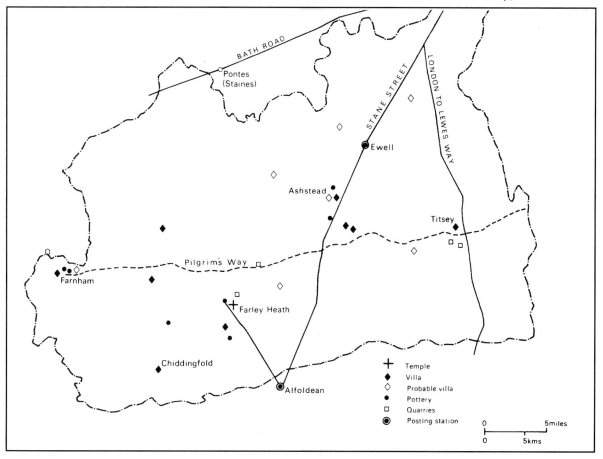

Although comparatively small, the largest Roman town in 'Surrey' was the bridgehead settlement where the Roman roads of Watling Street and Stane Street converged on the south bank of the Thames to cross into Londinium on the site of present-day Southwark. This was a sandy area divided by streams with swamps to east and west. Excavation of bomb-damaged buildings and later investigation has revealed a Roman occupation along the riverside and a ribbon development bordering the two main roads. This urban growth appears to be of the Flavian period (A.D. 69-79). Settlement on the excavated sites is covered by dark silt layers, presumably laid down by floodwaters which mark the period of rising sea level from the early fourth century. The neglect of river embankments during the very disturbed third century in Roman Britain may have been a contributory factor in the decline of the south bank.

14 *Well executed 'dog and stag' relief-patterned tile die stamp, Ashtead Roman Villa (after A.W.G. Lowther).*

The villas of Surrey are not as large or as opulent as those of Kent and Sussex, but at Ashtead was a corridor-type house of at least thirteen rooms, connected to Stane Street by a flint road. Here it is archaeologically possible to find skilled craftsmen in the late first century A.D. making box flue tiles for the villa's heating system, exquisitely impressed with the tiler's elaborate trademark by means of patterns cut in soft stone or a wooden cylindrical die-stamping roller sheathed in bronze. At the Rapsley villa in Ewhurst was a tile factory and the Titsey villa possessed a fulling mill. The potters of the river Wey district near Farnham were noted for coarse wares. Thus Surrey early began its long history as a workshop. The recession in these industries discernible in the third century A.D. is probably related to the decline of London as a trading centre.

The Stane Street flung across the Weald is the greatest monument to the Roman practical genius in Surrey. With the aid of aerial photography and detailed fieldwork, I.D. Margary traced its entire length between Chichester and London. It is well engineered to secure the shortest route allowed by the lie of the land. Finds along the road at Dorking, Epsom, Ewell and Tooting indicate important sites of human occupation by *c*.70 A.D. Near Ockley, Stane Street remains in use as a fine raised causeway across deep Weald clay. A splendid derelict section is traceable on a wider *agger* across Mickleham Downs between the Mole Valley and Epsom.

3

Saxon Surrey

It was formerly supposed, following 19th-century historians, that the Saxons migrated from across the North Sea to a virtually uninhabited country, having displaced or exterminated the conquered peoples of the Roman cantons. It is now accepted that the Saxons did not occupy Britain in the very large numbers assumed by earlier historians and consequently the scenario has been generally abandoned and scholars now conjecture a quite different course of events. Roman Surrey, as other parts of Roman Britain, was in a rather run-down state in the early fifth century but it was full of Romano-Britons with many good roads, villages, villas and a fair notion of civilised life. The Saxons migrated in numbers too few for extensive land-taking and the notion that the Saxons were the 'makers' of Surrey, or indeed any other part of southern England, is now discarded and the chequered landscape of the present day is seen to have its roots in a gradual evolution from as far back as the Iron Age, or even the Bronze Age. It has also been suggested that the great feudal estates governed from a single headquarters first revealed in later Saxon Surrey and elsewhere may not necessarily be the work of Germanic invaders, as had formerly been assumed, but an inheritance from an administrative system based earlier on Roman villas and before that on Iron-Age hill-forts. Unfortunately, the historical and archaeological evidence for the period A.D. *c*.400-*c*.600 is so weak at present that we cannot understand the course of events of this period. Saxon settlement began in the early fifth century when the leaders of Roman Britain called in Saxon federate troops to defend them against the Picts. Later the Saxons rebelled and took over control of some areas. Graves recording the earliest signs of Saxon migration into Surrey appear to have been English colonies assisting the Romano-British inhabitants of London to secure the city against the flanking advance of other bands of English marauders (fig.15). Sites at Ham, Mitcham and Croydon, for example, have yielded military-type metalwork of this period.

The degree to which later contact between Saxons and Romano-Britons occurred and the extent to which continuity between late Roman 'Surrey' and Saxon Surrey took place are still uncertain. Very interesting are place-names which may suggest a survival of Romano-British Christianity such as the lost *eccles hamme* noted by Blair near Bisley and St Martha's Hill which Morris believed is derived from *martyrum*. Rob Poulton has noted

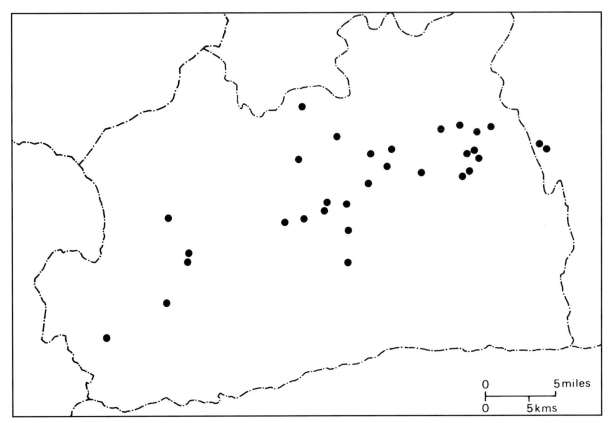

15 *The early Saxon burial sites (after Audrey Meaney,* A Gazetteer of early Anglo-Saxon Burial Sites *[1964]).*

disc brooches and other styles which have been explained as native fashions adopted by Germanic immigrants. At a Croydon cemetery yielding a large number of Saxon objects four contemporary Roman pots were also found, suggesting the possibility that the Saxon graveyard was a successor to a native one. At present there is an extreme rarity of evidence for direct settlement continuity between Romano-British and Saxon in Surrey but Poulton has suggested a partition agreed between the Saxons and Romano-Britons, as Martin Welch has suggested for Sussex, on the grounds that the Godalming-Chertsey-Woking area may have stayed British for a time when the rest of the present county was already under Saxon control.

The name *Surrey*, spelt by the Venerable Bede as *Sudre ge* and in Domesday Book as *Sudrie*, contains two highly significant English elements which throw some light on these important new events. The second syllable of the name is derived from Old English *ge*, akin to German *gau*, meaning 'inhabitants of a district or region'. The first element means 'south'. The name Surrey means therefore the 'south region'. Geographically the meaning is plain. It suggests that Surrey was originally the southern district of a Middle Saxon kingdom which included Middlesex ('Norrey') coterminous across the Thames. There is no written tradition to support this and at present no definite corroborative archaeological evidence, but it is perhaps noteworthy that the goods excavated from the early fifth-century graves of Saxon federates in the Wandle valley around Croydon and Mitcham differ stylistically from those across the Medway in Kent, but resemble those found on the north and west sides of London. Nevertheless, it is impossible to define precisely the area which later came to be occupied by the Saxon whose early place-names are so conspicuous in the valleys of the Wandle, Mole and Wey. The phonology of the place-names of eastern Berkshire suggests that the English people in this wooded area were of Surrey stock: for example, the people from whom Wokingham in Berkshire were named are almost certainly the same group referred to in the Surrey place-name of Woking and it is possible that the district around Sonning, and perhaps even further west around Reading, once formed part of the Surrey section of the Middle Saxon kingdom. Reference to the 1:50000 Ordnance Map will indicate that the county boundary of Surrey against Sussex is generally drawn in favour of the latter and is artificial, neither following the headwaters of the Arun nor the watershed of the Weald. Also significant are the existence of many place-names ending in -*fold* straddling both sides of the Surrey-Sussex border. These initially denoted summer pastures for swine. Their distribution inevitably invites speculation as to the location of the parent villages responsible for the hiving off of men and animals into the Wealden forest. The *folds* may well commemorate the summer swinecotes of South Saxon (Sussex) origin.

From the beginnings of recorded history, Saxon Surrey was neither a separate kingdom like Kent, Sussex and Wessex, nor a stable element within a kingdom. Instead it was in the words of John Blair 'a frontier territory buffeted between the southern English rulers'. As early as A.D. 568 Ceawlin of Wessex fought against Ethelbert of Kent and drove him back eastwards. For nearly three centuries more Surrey remained in the same unstable state. In 666 the sub-king of Surrey had to obtain the consent of King Wulfhere of Mercia, the Midland kingdom, before founding the Abbey of St Peter at Chertsey and in 672 land was granted to the Chertsey minster by Frithuwold, a sub-king of Mercia. Frithuwold himself appears to have been a member of the Mercian dynasty and not native to Surrey. By the late 680s Caedwalla of Wessex had decisively turned the power balance in favour of Wessex and had secured the Farnham area. A papal decree of *c*.708 locates the minsters of Bermondsey and Woking in the province of the West Saxons but Surrey subsequently fell into the overlordship of Offa of Mercia who confirmed a grant to Woking church. In 825 the men of Surrey, Kent, Sussex and Essex submitted to Ecgbert of Wessex and Surrey became decisively part of the kingdom of the West Saxons. It is probable that during the next few decades it finally gained cohesion as a West Saxon shire with boundaries much as they remained until modern times for several of the kings of the House of Wessex were crowned at Kingston-upon-Thames. When Edward the Elder re-organised the West Saxon sees in 909 he left Surrey in the Winchester diocese where it remained until the 20th century.

Blair's work on the key administrative institutions in Surrey is very relevant to the current belief in the continuity in the landscape, for the most

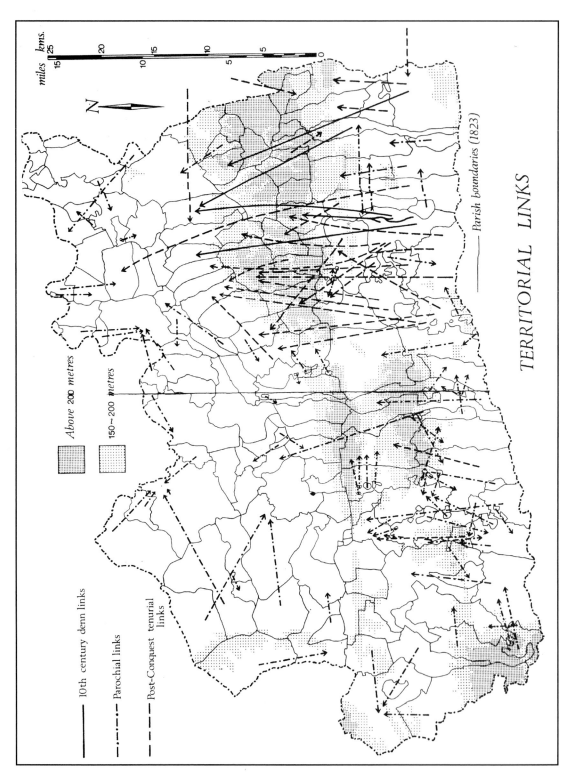

miles kms.

Above 200 metres

150~200 metres

Parish boundaries (1823)

TERRITORIAL LINKS

10th century denn links

Parochial links

Post-Conquest tenurial links

16 *Territorial links between older and later settlement in Surrey (after Blair).*

important questions about survival and continuity have to do with the transference of power. The orderly, if complicated, administrative system centring on royal vills to which were owed dues and services, but with a recognisably similar system extending from Wales, through England into Scotland, suggests that at least for the northern part of Britain its origins are to be found in the pre-Saxon period, although there is at present no means of assessing its age. It is conceivable, therefore, that the -*ingham* and -*tun* place-names in Surrey are not primarily the result of Saxon colonisation and a devastated Romano-British administrative area but that they represent frontier settlements on land of dependent Romano-British stature and that the name of settlements was changed at some time during the Saxon take over and it was the English names that were committed to written record. Blair's work on the *regiones* shows that the transfer of organised areas of government from Britons to Saxons in Surrey could have readily arisen in an orderly manner without great bloodshed.

Blair has elucidated the system of Saxon landholding based on districts (*regiones*) focused on royal or episcopal estates, viz., those of Godalming, Woking, Kingston, Reigate, Wallington and Farnham. The later civil districts called Hundreds were based on these *regiones*. Each of these estates had numerous settlements apart from the headquarters together with lord's demesne and peasant farms, woods, common and marshes fragmented into a complex, interlocking, archipelago. In central and eastern Surrey manors have detached outliers in the Weald on the Kentish and Sussex models in a bewildering system of intersecting rights. It is uncertain whether this framework is Saxon or pre-Saxon in origin.

Blair has also thrown great light on the early religious organisation of Surrey. He has identified the earliest churches as minster churches founded by kings or bishops at important and administrative centres, typically comprising five to fifteen modern parishes, each minster having priests who had a responsibility for the whole area served by the minster. These minster churches were Chertsey, the oldest of all, Bermondsey, Farnham, Woking, Kingston, Godstone, Croydon, Godalming, Lambeth, Leatherhead, Southwark and Stoke, near Guildford. Blair has shown how Kingston minster parish had by the 12th century developed into a number of church dependencies (fig.17). The other minster churches similarly declined in importance during the 11th and 12th centuries.

Our knowledge of the daily life and settlement geography of Saxon Surrey during this Dark Age, and for generations to come, turns largely upon the topographical studies drawing upon the cumulative evidence of place-names and Saxon local land charters. These enable one to trace, however shadowy, the exploitation of the land and the process by which the Saxons transformed their setting of marsh, heath and forest into farmland during the six obscure but formative centuries between the first migrations of Saxons south of the Thames in the sixth century and the making of Domesday Book in 1086.

Broadly speaking, the colonisation in the Saxon period was from the most inviting to the most unfriendly soils, for pioneer farmers had occupied all the most accessible and workable soils by the end of the fifth century.

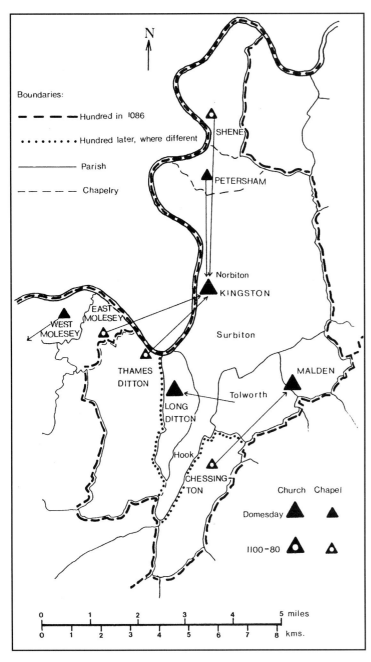

Place-names in O.E. *ham*, meaning a village community, a manor or a homestead, and O.E. *ham*, considered to have meanings of an enclosure or a meadow by a stream, are generally reckoned to belong to an early stratum of English names. The majority of these place-names in Surrey occur north of the Pilgrims' Way in districts which have always been inviting to settlement and which were probably cleared of woodlands during the Roman occupation and earlier.

Another indication of very early settlement is the several place-names which were given in south-west Surrey before the coming of Christianity in the late seventh century. These heathen names include Willey, near Farnham, whose O.E. form is derived from Old English *weoh*, an idol or shrine, and *leah*, a clearing. Such religious symbols were commonly established in natural clearings in woodland. It is also suggested that the place-names of neighbouring Thursley and Tuesley may have been clearings where the gods Thunor and Tiw were worshipped. The second element of Peper Harrow is from Old English *hearg*, a temple. Thunderfield in Horley may also indicate an open space where a shrine of Thunor was placed.

Another place-name especially interesting with regard to Surrey is Old English *ceart*, occurring only on the sands or sandstones, and surviving in the dialect of Kent and Surrey as 'chart'. It denotes 'rough, uncultivated land overgrown with gorse,

17 *Relationships between minster churches and chapels in Surrey, pre-Domesday to c.1180 (after Blair).*

broom, bracken and the like'. These 'wastes' were invariably outlying portions of manors centred on the Vale of Holmesdale.

Such place-name evidence is coarse-grained and still notoriously difficult to interpret with any degree of accuracy. If we now turn to some of the Saxon land charters we can begin to decipher the economic and social structure of some estates and their integrated nature. The King's farm or

I *The famous view from Richmond Terrace up the middle Thames valley, which has inspired painters and poets and aroused such international feeling that in 1902 it became the first view to be protected by an Act of Parliament. The new Thames Strategy aims to retain and enhance the view for the 21st century.*

II *Surrey in the early 19th century has been aptly described by David Watkins as 'an excited version of a "Capability Brown" park on the very grandest scale'. H.H. Parker's* The Wey *(1884), a scene near Elstead, is an example of how much of the natural bloom could still be captured by artists retaining a base in London.*

III *Helen Allingham, Sand-hills (1882). This view to Tennyson's Blackdown is still remarkably unspoiled and retains something of its former 'cottagey' character.*

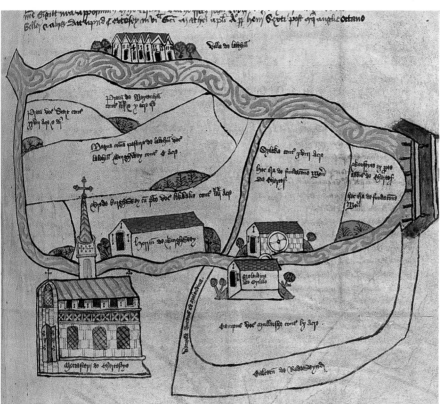

IV *A late 15th-century plan of Chertsey Abbey and its demesnes. The village of Laleham is depicted at the top: the Abbey is shown at the bottom. The barn at Burgheye, built by Abbot John Rutherwyk in 1315, is also shown, together with mills, a fish weir, a large common pasture and several fields. The Abbey Moat and Abbey River, an artificial cut across Thames meanders, were both large excavations requiring an impressive amount of manpower.*

estate of Kingston-upon-Thames was sited at a ford across the river and, uniquely in Surrey, its outlying, dependent farms were denoted *bartons*: Norbiton was the north *barton* and Surbiton the south *barton*. Battersea contained at least three distinct elements; the farmland at Battersea itself; the brushwood on Battersea Rise (O.E. *hris*, brushwood) and the swine pastures at Penge, a British name corresponding to the Welsh *pen* ('head') and *coed* ('wood'). In a charter of A.D. 957 we are told that the Penge woods were 'seven miles, seven furlongs and seven feet in circumference'.

The Surrey Weald

The most striking feature of the Saxon landscape of South-East England, however, must have been the wild and almost uninterrupted country which spread across the Wealds of Surrey, Kent and Sussex between the inward-facing North and South Downs. Over this huge tract the victory of man over an untamed nature was still to be won in early Saxon times. It was as a swine herd and cattle-drover that the Saxon first left his mark on the forest.

The first men inhabiting the unenclosed woods or wastes in Surrey may have been *drofmen*, drovers engaged in tending cattle, who, unlike other peasants, grew no corn and had no oxen for the plough. Such peasants, and also swineherds, would have divided their year between their 'winter house', their permanent abode in the village and the 'summer house' in the distant woodland pasture. The *drofmen* possibly took hurdles on their annual migration to the forest and by these means erected summer houses consisting only of a single room and a cattle-yard.

This organisation of the inhabited space in Saxon Surrey and the long-continued custom of herding swine and cattle into the Weald for summer pasture is still reflected with remarkable clarity by the surviving road system. It is readily observable that the general direction of the close net of by-roads is from north to south. On closer examination, it will be found that each of the villages and hamlets of the Vale of Holmesdale has a direct connection with places in the deep Surrey Weald. That some of these routes, or parts of them, have become totally unnecessary is indicated by their present unmetalled condition. If we now take, by way of example, the roads and trackways within the triangle bounded by Woking, Leatherhead and Horsham, many of these are traceable over quite remarkably long distances, running down from the North Downs into the heavy clays of the Weald. It is a road system which suggests that the local necessity of villagers in the Vale of Holmesdale was not so much connections between their neighbouring villages as between their village and the outlying woodland of the Weald. We are, in fact, examining the road pattern of a large number of anciently self-sufficing communities. It is a conscious design related to three main resources of each manor: the arable and meadow on the richer soils about the parent villages; the sheep pastures on Downs or heath, and the swine grazings in the Weald. This also explains the striking symmetrical distribution of rural settlement at the foot of the Chalk escarpment and along the edge of the Lower Greensand formation, for here the best soils were to be found. This gave rise to very long and narrow 'strip parishes' adapted for ecclesiastical administration. It also explains the archaic territorial characteristic of detached parishes in the Weald as outliers of parishes to the north.

The old pattern of Wealden 'outliers' can be instanced by reference to central Surrey. The scattered farmhouses of Newdigate parish are younger than its road, for the parish name probably means 'on Ewoodgate', i.e., on the road between Reigate and Rusper which passed through Ewood, a great woodland in the parish. In the earliest documents relating to Newdigate church it is designated a subordinate chapel, presumably dependent upon Reigate. Much of Burstow parish was originally part of the Archbishop of Canterbury's manor of Wimbledon and Thunderfield in Horley was a swine pasture of Sutton manor. Banstead had a Wealden outlier in Leigh. When the church of Capel (Old French *capelle*, a chapel) first appears in recorded history it is merely as a chapel-of-ease to Dorking. Oakwood was a detached part of Wotton and the status of its church has had a similar evolution to that of Capel. Much of Charlwood lay within the manor of Merstham, owned by monks of Christchurch, Canterbury. Horne was constituted as a separate parish as late as the reign of Queen Anne: until then it was a detached part of Bletchingley. Haslemere was originally dependent upon Chiddingfold, as the latter was at a more distant date to Godalming. Shere originally included Cranleigh. The men of these subordinate settlements would have been obliged originally to carry their dead for burial to the main church and to go there also to marry and to baptise their children. The steady development of chapelries into separate parishes during the later Middle Ages reflects the growing wealth and population of the Weald.

Many of these human habitations evolved from a stage of temporarily occupied huts or shelters associated with seasonal pastoral farming before they were permanently inhabited by farmers who cultivated land within ring-fenced fields. This evolution is one of the most characteristic of the Surrey Weald. The evidence for the change from one stage to the next is less than for successive stages of settlement. Very characteristic of the west Surrey Low Weald and the adjoining part of Sussex are the sites of large farmhouses and of Saxon and early Norman churches bearing the suffix *-fold* (O.E. *falod*). These *folds* are invariably found on the low swells of better-drained soil of a lighter texture and brown colour. They help to recall the ancient forest landscape and the earliest graziers because the word denotes staking off as pasture ground for a cattle (or swine) pen into which the animals would have been herded at night. The very general use of the suffix suggests that the Wealdsmen who pitched their *folds* in the openings within the woods were originally herders of animals rather than farmers. The *fold* was therefore the germ of a farm and, later still, often a village.

When the *folds* and also *dens* and *shots* (derived from O.E. *den* and *scydd*, meaning woodland pastures, especially for swine) passed into permanent occupation is one of the unresolved puzzles of Surrey history. We cannot answer the question with any assurance for whereas, for most parts

18 *Swine slaughtering (Corpus Christi Coll.).*

of England, Domesday Book provides some idea of the extent of the clearings at the end of the 11th century, the Surrey folios are not an adequate source of settlement history for they do not separately enumerate colonists in the outlying Wealden parts of manors based on its northern periphery. Yet circumstantial evidence that agriculture and settlement had made considerable headway in the Weald is impressive. Of special importance is the evidence that churches had been founded in Wealden parishes to serve the scattered community growing there. This evidence reinforces Lennard's injunction that 'we must not be too ready to fill the vacant spaces of the Domesday map with imagined woodland or marsh'. By the 1080s, most of the Weald land had been fully colonised, though population was doubtless very sparse. Settlements with names ending in -ley (*leah*) are definitely the result of Saxon woodland clearance. Eleven such settlements are recorded in Domesday Book: Bletchingley, Witley, Henley in Ash and the two Horsleys, East and West, had become extensive clearings and the nuclei of substantial manors.

Embryonic Towns

A world apart from the still raw Weald of Saxon times were the embryonic towns of the late Saxon period. Eashing, now a mere village, is on the site of a specially designated refuge (*burh*) against the Danes, established probably by King Alfred the Great *c*.880. This site has been identified with a cliff overlooking the present bridge across the river Wey. It proved a failure as a permanent settlement, Guildford, in the superior position at a convenient crossing of the Wey, superseding it. The Domesday entry for this town notes that 'King William has 75 sites wherein dwell 175 men', and thus already Guildford had a population of about 700 people. It was certainly in existence by the 10th century since a mint is attested by a silver penny of Ethelred the Unready. An examination of the town plan of Guildford by O'Connell and Poulton has clarified that most of the town was a single act of late-Saxon town planning, the area near the late Saxon church of St Mary being notably older. A mint was also established at Godalming before the Norman Conquest, indicating an important status. Kingston-upon-Thames was distinguished as a town by its royal residence. Poulton has suggested that it originated as a *burh* refuge as there are signs of rectangular planning east of the site of the medieval bridge.

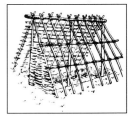

19 *Saxon weaver's hut formerly at the Weald and Downland Museum..*

The leading Saxon town, as in Roman times, was Southwark, first mentioned in the *Burghal Hidage* as *Suthringa geweorche*, 'the defensive work of the men of Surrey'. By the 11th century, Southwark had grown into a large town. The intimate connection between many Surrey villages and the essential life of London in the 11th century is indicated by dwellings in London and Southwark appurtenant to rural manors. In Domesday Book these properties are confined to manors south and south-west of London. Not only were nearer manors such as Lambeth, Bermondsey, Mortlake, Merton and Long Ditton in possession of property in the City of London, but so also were more distant manors such as Bletchingley,

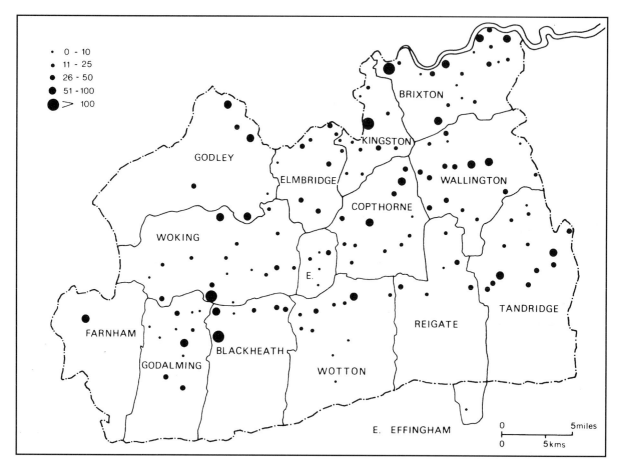

20 *Recorded population in the Domesday Survey. Based on the data provided by John Morris in* Domesday Book: Surrey *(Phillimore, 1976). The largest symbols need to be spread out, as it were, by eye over the surrounding blank areas. The manors are grouped into the old administrative units of Hundreds.*

Godstone (Walkingstead), Banstead and Walton-on-the-Hill. The correspondence between this distribution and the map of Dark-Age pagan burial sites (p.28) is so close that it is difficult not to believe that the defence of London is an explanation.

The data in Domesday Book provide a rough measure of Surrey's relative economic development at that time. Blair concludes that Surrey was then one of the more lightly settled parts of lowland England. Only the manors near London were relatively well-populated, while the Windsor Forest area was among the few districts of conspicuously low density in southern England. This is strikingly different from the economy of Kent and Sussex notwithstanding their extensive woods and wastes, because of the strong development and relatively dense population of their coastal districts.

4

Medieval Farming and Woodmanship

Although late Saxon settlement had been considerable in the Surrey Weald extensive intervening wastes were still lacking agricultural colonists in the early 13th century. At Ruckenham, as elsewhere, peasants were taking up small parcels of land as woodland clearings ('breaches' or *rudings*). Many of the occupiers took as surnames the name of their smallholding: Henry de la Breche, Richard le Brechere, Walter atte Rud, etc. As early as the 1320s two water mills had been built. A wide range of handicrafts developed at Ruckenham for many of the later colonists, short of land, grappled with the local raw materials of timber, clay, iron, water-power, wood and hides. The wood-crafts of coopering, turnering and tanning are well represented by occupation names. Numerous of the woodland clearers, for example at Ruckenham, were part-time farmer-artisans, including Godefrid le Verer (glassmaker), Thomas and Robert Faber, possibly, as their name suggests, smiths or iron-makers, Walter le Chaboner (charcoal burner), and Thomas le Denere, a holder of 'pot-lands', i.e. places of pottery manufacture. Nearby Oakwood, a remote part of Wotton manor, was also developing at this time into a hamlet-community with expanding *ruds* and handicrafts. Ian Nairn wrote of the 'unforgettable situation' of Oakwood church (originally a chapel of Wotton) surrounded by its still thick woods, patchwork fields and that these tangible signs of unspoilt medieval character still give 'the impression of frontier uneasiness, a refreshing thing to find in Surrey'. An interesting feature of early Surrey society is the large number of slaves (*servi*) recorded in Domesday Book. It is possible to envisage a process by which slaves were being placed on outlying woodland in the Weald and cultivated demesnes before the practice began of granting land to peasants to do the same work.

The Weald proved a difficult farming region. The intractability of its cold, thin clay soils became a by-word, and, in addition, soils were deficient in phosphate, calcium, potassium and nitrogen. Agriculture was a matter of considerable expense and difficulty and, on account of the miry roads, large areas were scarcely accessible for much of the year. Medieval cropping was on a basis of convertible (alternate) husbandry under which system a relatively small proportion of the arable was cultivated on quasi-permanent basis with the aid of generous manuring. The remaining fields underwent short bouts of continuous cultivation and then rested for a similar period to recuperate.

Unquestionably, the principal manure used for land improvement was marl. A direct application of lime from the nearest source along the distant Chalk rim of the Weald became practicable only with the more abundant horses and wagons of the 17th century. The medieval farmer, accustomed to dear carriage and cheap labour, made the marl pit do the duty of a lime kiln. A pit was dug in the corner of almost every field and farmers winched up calcareous clay found in subordinate beds below the top-soil and spread it over each field before ploughing about once in 20 years.

Nearly all the Wealdsman raised he consumed at home. Probably only his annual crop of calves broke out of the circle of subsistence, for beasts were marketable on the hoof. He worked his small farm with the aid of his family and farms to this day often bear the names of their 13th- or 14th-century occupiers.

Another developing district was the Royal Forest of Windsor, formerly a wild tract of country nine miles wide, and extending across 17 parishes in north-west Surrey and the adjoining part of Berkshire. Forest used in this sense was neither a botanical nor a geographical term, but a legal one. The word is derived from the Latin *foris*, meaning outside, and was applied to land where the Common Law of England did not pertain. The territory 'afforested' in the case of the Forest of Windsor was largely heathland developed on the sterile sands of the Bagshot Sands formation. A document of considerable topographical interest is the Forest Regarder's rent roll of 1372. It begins by detailing the specific landmarks along the boundary of the Forest which have been identified in a recent perambulation. These are of particular interest, because the perambulation is one of the earliest authentic descriptions of the Surrey landscape that we possess.

21 *Medieval tithe barn.*

Although the progressive clearing of woodland in the early Middle Ages was the main process of landmaking in Surrey, the reclamation of the heathland in the Forest of Windsor was also an important process in the development of its peasant society. There were many surviving areas of opportunity for the colonist. In the late 13th century the Crown empowered its Constable of Windsor to enclose and lease out for cultivation all the old sheepwalks near villages within the Forest and peasants secured the right to fence meadow and fields with a growing hedge in these parts of the Forest. The Abbots of Chertsey and Westminster conferred similar facilities. At Pyrford the Abbot of Westminster had between 160-170 tenants in 1330, 70 of them cottagers or smallholders, and the swelling rent roll suggests that the village was growing right up to the Black Death. On the Abbey of Chertsey's estate Chobham and other vills were growing at the same period. Within the bounds of the Royal Forest itself Chobham, Frimley, Horsell, Ottershaw, Pirbright, Pyrford and Worplesdon were also filling up with small-holders. Most of the cottagers cultivated their tiny plots more like kitchen gardens than farms, sowing a little winter and summer corn in regular succession without respite. It is unlikely that the soil could have borne good crops for more than a few years at a time with the little manure available.

One of these little peasant farmers is immortalised in the records of the Abbey of Chertsey. When his holding was confiscated by the Abbot because he was farming it badly in 1332, William de Brok of Chobham owned four oxen, seven steers, two cows, two-and-a-half quarters of winter wheat and five quarters of oats—just enough perhaps to feed a family on good white bread and to earn a little money in the market place. As his holding could not support all his livestock, William de Brok would have run his animals on the common and also cut fern for litter, later to be applied as manure to his meadows. He would also have prepared his pork by smoke strongly impregnated with the pungent aroma of burning peat, also produced by the Forest, and his evening light was probably simply a rush dipped in grease. In every way William de Brok is a forerunner of the race of 'broom-squires' of the 19th century.

One way of tracing the most anciently farmed Surrey countryside is by examining the evidence afforded by the hedgerows themselves. Dr. Max Hooper has suggested that there may be a correlation between the age of a hedge and a number of different shrub species growing in it. The count of the shrubs (as defined in a standard list and along a 30-yard stretch of hedge) gives the approximate age of the hedge in centuries. The reasons are complex and little understood, and readers are referred to the work of Pollard, Hooper and Moore (1974). The very old hedges were commonly planted on a wide earthbank bordered by a ditch acting as a deep water run to carry water off upland fields in wet seasons.

It is too early to judge whether Hooper's hypothesis is applicable to Surrey. Sample tests suggest that some hedge counts are correlated with age. The hedges bordering Roundals Lane, Hambledon (the old road to Petworth), for example, average about eight to nine species which could give them an origin about A.D. 1000, which is quite acceptable in the light of the general documentary evidence. Again, the species growing on a fine hedge near Shoelands, Puttenham, which is in older settled country, number up to eleven, but this has been managed until recently to produce a full range of timber for local wood workers (principally oak, ash and hazel). Many other Surrey hedges have been similarly planted up for the timber trade and on large estates game shelters and ornament explain hedgerows, supporting up to 14 and, exceptionally, 16 'countable' species.

22 *Medieval tree-pruner (Ms. Corpus Christi Coll, 285).*

The wood-clearing techniques of pioneer farmers have also contributed to the present landscape in another way. Unlike other districts enclosed directly from the wild, many fields were not bounded by narrow, crooked hedgerows, but by strips of woodland up to 33ft. wide, locally known as shaws or *rewes*. Such shaws certainly formed part of the medieval landscape for field-names incorporating this element are recorded from the 13th century. William Marshall attributed this local custom to the exceptionally large nursery of oak, ash, hedge-maple and hazel trees needed by Wealden farmers who supplied markets in fuel (including charcoal for the iron industry) and shipbuilding timber. Moreover, in a region where soil was mediocre and land cheap and plentiful, the shaw provided a fence with a minimum of effort and expense. The little fields of the pioneer farmer—

typically only two to four acres in size—gave hardly room for the plough and were often too cold and poor to be ploughed with profit. They were, however, considered by early farmers as ideal for livestock, affording good shelter and a series of 'paddocks' for use in rotation. This 'old way of very small fields for the stock' persisted into the mid-19th century when under-draining led to the grubbing up of many hedgerows, and destruction since has been very considerable. Yet fossilised medieval fields still exist in frag-mentary patchworks.

In the 13th and 14th centuries the valuation placed for fiscal purposes upon land of a deceased major landowner (contained in *Inquisitiones post mortem*) provides illuminating information as to the use of the land in Surrey at this period. Used with caution, they show how practically-minded farmers responded to their environmental burdens or opportunities. The maximum efficiency of agriculture of most of medieval England was prob-ably reached under a three-course rotation of wheat, barley or oats, and fallow, thus leaving one-third of the farmland almost idle in any given year. In some specially favoured districts such as the coastlands of Norfolk, north Kent and coastal Sussex, fallowing was reduced and corn yields were higher. Sheep flocks in these coastal districts were large.

It is significant that much of Surrey failed to reach even the intensity of land use based on the standard three-course system. In the Weald, arable farming was greatly extended during the 13th century, but it sharply contracted following the severe reduction in population as a result of the Black Death of 1348-9 and much land presumably lapsed back to wood-land and scrub for want of a market. On the lean sandy soils of the Lower Greensand formation, only a half of the field acreage, or even less, was apparently cultivated at any one time. The proportion of arable rose on Downland soils, but it was of low value because of its dry, hilly and stony nature. It is only near London, on the richer soils of the Thames valley, and also in the Vale of Holmesdale below the Chalk escarpment in the middle of the county, that manors achieved something like a two-thirds use of arable land. One or two estates will be singled out for special mention. For Wotton, near Dorking, the surviving *Inquisitiones* record an intensity of land use ranging from a 'low' of only 40 arable acres out of 200 in 1300 to a 'high' of 80 acres in 1282. This estate straddled the Vale of Holmesdale, but included much rough Chalkland and sandy heath. It can probably be regarded as a microcosm of Surrey because the crop yields on other estates, for example, those of the Bishop of Winchester at Farnham and Esher, were not greatly higher. Since there is no evidence that the crop yields of the peasantry differed to any extent from those of the larger landowners we must assume a lower level of agricultural pro-duction in Surrey than from its neighbouring counties.

In the Weald most of the farmland was probably taken into separate occupation from the very first clearance of the wood. The lord's demesne in the Weald, and generally in Surrey, was consolidated into separate par-cels and farmed separately. The peasants' land outside the Weald was apparently dispersed in common fields, but its enclosure into small hedged fields had begun by the early 15th century and when the earliest estate maps become available in the late 16th and early 17th centuries only fragmentary common field systems survived in Surrey. The reason for the early enclosure was probably the necessity for a flexible farming system on soils equally suitable for arable and pasture. Common fields survived longest where the soils were light enough for sheep folding, the cheapest and most effective way of manuring arable.

If Surrey was a place of medieval abundance, it was in its store of fruit and forest trees. Regarding fruit and gardening, the art of horticulture and fruit-growing had by the 14th century already made Surrey a land of gardens. In the Weald fruit-growing was practised (for subsistence purposes) on a considerable scale. For want of good barley (an unsuitable crop on the heavy soils), an orchard for cider and apple-butter was early planted on every farm. Elsewhere in Surrey the 'great gardens' attached to manor houses were remarkably well stocked with fruit trees, and the dry, stony soils of the Chalk were plentifully furnished with vineyards. Throughout medieval Surrey, but particularly in the middle and south, cider-drinking was a great institution and all the manor farms belonging to Merton College, Oxford, possessed a cider-press.

Woodmanship

The rapidly-expanding English economy of the 13th and early 14th centuries greatly increased the demand for timber and fuel. This led to a changing attitude about the remaining Surrey woodland. Men became studious less to cut down trees than to plant them. It became an increasingly precious resource which needed conservation. The Church and the great estates set an example. John de Rutherwyk, Abbot of Chertsey from 1307 to 1346 (whose unflagging zeal and prudence in estate management must have been hard to rival) sowed acorns and planted young oaks in his hedgerows and groves, doubtless to supplement woods that had been too heavily exploited. Great timber beams from the Abbey's estate can still be seen in the fine churches of Great Bookham and Egham, the finest monuments remaining in the present landscape of this great abbot. We can also trace attempts to protect and tend trees as crops in the form of enclosed coppices for firewood, charcoal, hurdles, fencing, etc. This involved the regular felling near the ground level of hazel, alder and other broad-leaved species which reproduced from fresh shoots from the stump (or stool). By the early 13th century in Surrey, and probably from a much earlier period, the principle of cutting this underwood on rotation of six to 12 years was widely practised.

At Farleigh near Croydon another thread of woodmanship can be unravelled. This was the practice of growing standards (mature oak and beech trees) above the lower storey of coppice. This was the traditional Surrey system of tree-growing to meet the demands of firewood and charcoal for London and also of timber for shipbuilding and building construction. Farleigh was an estate of Merton College, Oxford, and from its

23 *Threshing (Corpus Christi Coll.).*

documents its officials are shown to be very attentive to efficient woodland management in the 14th and 15th centuries, not basically different from principles practised today. The prime object of the coppice-with-standards system is to ensure a constant supply of well-developed standard trees of different ages in the same wood, so as to produce the highest possible sustained yield of suitable timber. By 1487 the College officials were specifying the number of standards which were to be left at each cutting and stipulating the kind of cattle-proof fence which was to be erected around the cut-over ground. It was the well-managed forestry on such English estates that influenced the later Tudor legislation, helping to make good forestry in the realm more universal.

24 *Medieval floor tiles produced (mostly in yellow and brown) at Chertsey Abbey. They are widely regarded as the finest ever made in England.*

5

The Early Medieval Church

William of Malmesbury, one of the greatest contemporary historians of the Anglo-Norman age, observed that: 'With their arrival the Normans breathed new life into religious standards which everywhere in England had been declining, so that you may see in every village, town and city churches and monasteries rising in a new style of architecture ...'. During the years 1030-1130 Surrey shared in this prodigious outburst of local church building activity on a scale as to justify borrowing from a later period the term 'Great Rebuilding' (Blair). The most striking expansion of churches was due to the rapid opening-up of the Weald for human settlement. As former swine pastures emerged as farmed communities they were provided with daughter churches by the parent settlements. Hambledon is the only one mentioned in Domesday Book: Leigh, Chivington, Crowhurst and Burstow soon followed. Blair has noted that in south-west Surrey four churches provide especially interesting evidence of church building. Churches at Hascombe and Godalming, daughters respectively of Shalford and Godalming minster and those of Cranleigh and Alfold, daughters, respectively, of East Shalford, eight miles northwards and Shere, have each virtually identical primary ground plans, viz., standard two-cell churches built to common dimensions in a late Saxon style.

Another socio-economic process which accounts for the proliferation of new churches was the proliferation of small manors after the Norman Conquest, in each of which the new lord of the manor tended to build a church for his own and his tenants' use. This is notable across the dip-slope of the Downs at Cuddington, Ashtead, Little Bookham, Fetcham, Effingham, Farleigh, Tatsfield, Caterham and Walton-on-the-Hill. Many of these proprietary churches are very small and contiguous to manor house sites. Some were so humble as to suggest they were built purely for household use, as at Chaldon and Headley. Religious houses also responded vigorously by providing churches for their tenants as on the Chertsey Abbey estate where churches were built at Egham, Thorpe, Cobham, East Clandon and Weybridge; Westminster Abbey likewise built churches on its manors at Pyrford, Horsell, Wandsworth, Battersea and Morden; Lewes Priory built a chapel for the emerging settlement at Capel (i.e. *Capella*). In all these places local churches had been conspicuously absent before the mid-12th century.

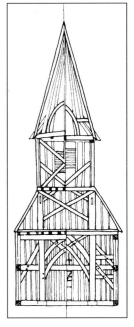

25 *Fifteenth-century wooden tower and spire, St Peter's Church, Newdigate (after Surrey Vernacular Architecture Group).*

26 Thursley Church: unusual and exceptionally lavish use of oak timber in construction.

Many former minsters had chapels of later foundation, e.g. Kingston with four chapelries of Petersham, Sheen, Thames Ditton and East Molesey (dependent on Kingston until 1769). The area served from Farnham similarly only acquired chapels in the 12th century. These local churches mark the decline of the minster churches considered on p.31.

Surrey churches are distinguished by the amount of wood used in their construction, appropriate in a county full of good timber but lacking in good stone and thinly inhabited by people in the past. Only Essex has a greater heritage of timber churches. The skill of the medieval carpenter is abundantly evident in the elaborate timber bell-towers or turrets constructed in the 14th and 15th centuries. The Wealden churches of Burstow, Horley, Horne, Leigh and Newdigate were all provided with ingenious timber towers in this period. At Leigh and Horne, the medieval tower has been replaced by a later structure. The timber tower of Burstow is a splendid piece of medieval carpentry, largely unrestored, retaining massive beams and posts hewn from locally-grown oak. Burstow still retains some of its former aspect as a woodland clearing before the Norman Conquest. One can enjoy in the churchyard the cool shade of broad-foliaged trees that melt gradually into woodland, like a garden into a wilderness. Unfortunately, the beautifully warm local sandstone of the church interior was plastered over in the heavy-handed 'restoration' of the church in 1882. A framed watercolour by A.A. Sykes placed in the church discloses its former beauty. When this modern plaster is scraped off, Burstow will again be a fine specimen of a simple Wealden church. The tower of Horley is of similar construction and date, possibly built by the same craftsmen as that of Burstow. Newdigate's massive double-braced corner posts support brilliantly contrived timber-work, though rather over-restored. Thursley, formerly a chapel-of-ease of Witley, is famous for its lofty octagonal wooden steeple which has risen on four unusual corner posts from the centre of the nave since the 15th century. Hascombe and Hambledon churches also possessed a wooden steeple in this position. Tandridge has a bell turret with a shingled spire on the west gable and smaller timber belfries still exist at Alfold, Bisley, Byfleet, Crowhurst, Dunsfold, Esher, Elstead, Thames Ditton and Warlingham, amongst others.

Surrey churches are also distinguished by their wooden screens. Compton church possesses the oldest such screen in England, a Norman example.

Many other beautiful medieval screens still survive, as at Gatton, West Horsley, Leatherhead, Nutfield, Reigate and Shere, but none of these can rival the exquisite craftsmanship of the cornice of the screen at Charlwood. In smaller and poorer churches, a single timber and plaster screen served as a division between nave and chancel as at Chelsham, Warlingham and Elstead.

Monastic Surrey

Waverley Abbey near Farnham holds a position of great importance in church history as the first Cistercian house in England, founded in 1128 by William Giffard, Bishop of Winchester with monks from L'Aumône, Normandy. These monks proved to be of commanding energy, resource and dedication, and exerted great influence on the general life of the English nation. Several of them became abbots of later Cistercian foundations. Eventually 128 Cistercian houses were founded in England, and Waverley, as the first of these, was recognised as the premier abbey of the order in this country.

27   *Waverley Abbey.*

The Cistercians practised the strict rule of not building houses in cities, castles or villages, and devoted their lives to meditation and scholarship. Waverley Abbey was beautifully sited on the banks of the river Wey two miles south of Farnham, on a sandy waste. This site was subject to recurrent floods in the 13th and early 14th centuries which damaged the conventual buildings and caused great hardship. The monastic church was moulded by the religious and architectural ideals of the high Middle Ages, a most creative epoch. This church was almost completely destroyed at the Dissolution of the Monasteries. Excavation has revealed a modest aisle-less architecture contrasting vividly with that of Rievaulx and Fountains in Yorkshire and it may thus reflect an older and short-lived tradition of the order. The conventual buildings when fully laid out embodied the principles of church planning in the 12th century. The precincts of the abbey were enclosed by walls and entered by several gateways giving access to various monastic buildings—infirmary, dormitory, lodgings of the abbot, guest house, refectory, brewhouse and stables—and all that was necessary for the self-contained life of the monks. These buildings were grouped about cloisters giving access to all the apartments and were the resort of the brethren during the hours set apart for meditation and study. This knowledge of the plan of Waverley is due to archaeological excavation, for the post-Reformation history of the abbey is one of centuries of neglect and ill-usage and

28   *Unpretentious Headley Church, typical of medieval churches in once sparsely inhabited parts of Surrey. Pevsner (*Buildings of Surrey*) described the present church built on the site of the demolished older church as 'A harsh conjunction: nave and chancel, 1855, by Salvin and appalling: tower 1859 by Street, and not bad, if hard.'*

29 *Surviving ruins of the Guest House, Waverley Abbey. Very little of the abbey church and little of the Common Room and of the abbey church remains. The upper storey still towering as a gable on the Guest House was a dormitory.*

30 *Bermondsey Abbey, remnant of the tower.*

little now survives above ground. Most of the building stone was robbed for fine new houses. Even since Aubrey's visit at the end of the 17th century the ruins have become much less extensive: 'Within the walls of the abbey were sixty acres ... here also remain walls of a fair church, the walls of the cloisters and some part of the cloisters themselves ... here was also a handsome chapel larger than that of Trinity College in Oxford ... the Hall was very spacious and noble ...'. Bestowed on Waverley were numerous endowments of land, much of it virgin wasteland, some of which the monks reclaimed and which became the economic basis of the monks' life. Distant properties were exploited as sub-stations called granges at, for example, Leigh, Tongham, Neatham, near Alton, and Wanborough. Despite this its properties were not highly valued, and in 1536, when the annual value of Waverley was assessed at under £200, it was suppressed by Thomas Cromwell as one of the lesser monasteries.

The Abbey of St Peter of Chertsey was a Benedictine foundation of A.D. 666 which had the distinction of being the oldest religious house in Surrey. It suffered terrible devastation at the hands of the Danes in the late ninth century, when the abbot and all his monks were slaughtered. The house was re-colonised from Abingdon and a new church was raised. It then became one of the largest and most influential of English monasteries. The Abbey's records are fullest for the first half of the 14th century when they exemplify the administrative ability of Abbot John de Rutherwyk (1307-46) which has already been noted. The Abbey's rôle as a vigorous coloniser of the sandy heaths bordering the Forest of Windsor is also very significant. The efficient administration of this great house in the 15th century is evidenced by the unique survival of a map of its demesne land, the earliest known in England.

6

Living in Medieval Town and Countryside

A prominent feature of the Wealden landscape was the moated homestead. Almost each parish has vestiges of several moated sites, still imperfectly surveyed and gazetteered. In Burstow an unusually large number are recorded. There are six definite sites (Old Lodge, Burstow Lodge, Rede Hall, Crullings, Cognans Farm, and a site in the grounds of the present Rectory) and two further possible sites—Burstow Park and Dowlands Farm. Three sites have been noted in the parish of Horley and three sites are known in Horne. Distribution tends to bear out the thesis that moated sites were manor houses, but 'the relation between topography and manorial records is at best only tenuously understood', writes one recent worker. The moated site in the Rectory grounds at Burstow is the only Surrey site to be excavated. It yielded pottery tentatively dated to the 14th century and other archaeological evidence suggested that it had been occupied from the late 13th down to the end of the 14th century. Unfortunately, deep garden-raking had destroyed almost all traces of the building that stood on the site. The location and small size of the moat suggests that it was the site of an earlier rectory. Apart from this hardly any scientific excavation has been done to record the unseen structure of moated sites.

To a remarkable degree medieval timber-framed buildings in Surrey have survived in the present landscape. The Domestic Buildings Research Group founded in Surrey in 1970 by Joan M. Harding has identified, so far, nearly 500 open-hall houses, of which 67 examples were built before 1400 and the remainder in the 15th century. The basic type of dwelling comprised an open-roofed hall with central hearth in which cooking was done as well as meals taken, smoke finding its way out through unglazed windows set as high as possible in the walls. The master's end of the hall communicated with the parlour, above which was the principal bedroom, used also by womenfolk during the day. At the other end was a cross-passage with doors at either end with side doors opening into a pantry and storeroom, above which there was an upper floor room. Timber, which was then abundant, was the normal material used, with thatch for the roof. The well was placed some nine feet or so outside the back door which was in line with the front door. Manor houses were built in the same style but often had a wing, or wings. The smallest surviving houses of two bays had an open hall and one bay with a roof over. The detail and quality of the

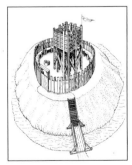

31 *A reconstruction of an early 12th-century motte and bailey castle at Abinger. Excavation has shown it to consist of a timber tower within a palisade on top of an artificial mound surrounded by a moat. Its form was close to depictions in the Bayeux Tapestry.*

47

32 *A former open-hall house at Shere.*

carpentry varied: superior houses had chamfers and stops round the wall-plates. Not until *c.*1500 were efforts made to control the smoke from the open hearth and houses were then being built with one bay of the hall ceiled over. The main method of roofing was by the use of a crown post which had a collar purlin extending the length of the roof under the collars, a dramatic central feature. In western Surrey carpenters tended to adopt a different structure, a clasped-purlin roof with two queen-struts up to a collar. Often a medieval house facing the road or church had an external jetty to increase the space in the bedroom. Some had an internal jetty of the main bedroom over the hall which not only increased the size of the room but provided under-floor warmth from the hall.

The finest achievement in timber-framed building is 'the Wealden'. This had a higher and wider hall with end bays jettied outwards so as to carry a continuous plate-beam supporting the hall rafters of the hall-front which were relieved of thrust. The overall effect was to impress passers-by or visitors and the lavish and lovely use of timber and moulding adds greatly to the charm of these houses. Typically they were the homes of wealthy clothiers and yeomen and their fewness in Surrey compared with Kent, and even Sussex, is a sign that Surrey was not a wealthy county in the 14th and 15th centuries.

A detailed account of expenses incurred in the rebuilding in 1497 by Merton College of its manor-house at Thorncroft throws much light on building operations of the time and it is also an important historical record of architectural change. Twelve loads of hewn timber were sent from

Newdigate and seven from Leigh, both in the Weald, and a further 16 from Chessington: these places were neighbouring properties of the College. An extra payment was made to the Chessington carters whose loads had stuck fast in the mire, and supplies from Newdigate took two days to cover the six miles to Leatherhead for the same reason. From Leigh, Ockley and Little Bookham came six oak trees, each as gifts to the Warden and Fellows. Forty loads of flint stones and 7,000 tiles were amongst other building materials used. The building work included the construction of two 'chimnenes'; the lofting over of the hall to provide a set of rooms on the upper floor; and also an 'outlay', i.e., a wing at ground level. Salt was procured for the hearth, presumably as a lining to prevent soot adhering to the sides of the chimney. Here we have the first recorded example in the county of the new fashion in the building for comfort which was to gather in its greatest momentum in the reign of Elizabeth I.

33 *Medieval household furniture (after Gertrude Jekyll).*

Although Guildford was a Saxon royal manor, the west Surrey refuge against the Danes in the 10th century was Eashing, perhaps because it was considered more naturally defendable. Nevertheless, by the late 11th century Guildford had emerged as the main town in the western part of the county, and in the 12th and 13th centuries it was to enjoy prosperity as an important royal residence. Henry III and Edward I transacted much state business from the castle. The shell of the square keep is still well preserved on its partly artificial mound. The street topography of old Guildford suggests conscious town planning in the Saxon or early Norman period, the outline of which is basically unmodified to this day. The small medieval town was a parallelogram less than a quarter mile from east to west and about a furlong in length. Surrounding it was the 'king's dyke', a defensive ditch first mentioned in the Patent Rolls in 1274, but doubtless much older. The only principal street was High Street. This was intersected at regular intervals by narrow ways called gates, several of which still exist. By the early 14th century Guildford was a prosperous little town. The cloth industry flourished and a fair granted in 1308 on St Catherine's Hill (where the Pilgrims' Way crossed the Wey gap), supplemented its regular markets. The presence of royalty and statesmen attracted money-lending Jews, including one Joceus, described as 'Jew of Guildford', who was murdered and robbed by thieves. Preaching friars worked amongst the poor from their friary on the north-west outskirts of the town and a charitable hospital dedicated to St Thomas the Martyr was established to support the sick and elderly on the east edge of the town, on a site now occupied by mock Tudor shops at the junction of the London and Epsom roads.

From the earliest surviving borough records of Guildford (1514-46) we obtain glimpses of Surrey town life at the end of the Middle ages. A gild merchant regulated trade, and other courts controlled the everyday life of the town community. A court met every three weeks to curb the fraudulence of offending bakers who over-charged or gave short-weight, and that of alehouse keepers who adulterated their ale.

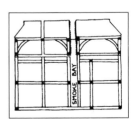

34 *Brittleware, Charlwood, a four-bay central smoke-bay house (after Surrey Vernacular Architecture Group).*

Periodically, the town's officers had to draft soldiers and food supplies needed for Henry VIII's military adventures and on at least one occasion

35 *Coat-of-arms, Borough of Guildford, comprising wool sacks.*

(November 1544) they were required by the government to counteract a serious danger of famine by regulating the flow of grain to market. Court officials were also obliged to assess citizens for state taxes and collect on behalf of the Tudor government the money due. The courts also strove, in typical medieval fashion, to exert an exclusive control in the sphere of the cloth trade by attempting to enforce apprenticeship regulations for fullers and shearmen. In matters of general trade they carefully regulated the operation of the markets. Not all dealers were town residents: one who had a regular 'stand' was one Tykenore, a tallow chandler from Wonersh. Like all other English towns of the period, Guildford was attempting to cleanse its streets by curbing the wanderings of stray pigs. The town officials also acted as administrators for debts, and inventories of debtors' goods are invaluable insights into early town life. Poor Elizabeth Charlys, owing rent and other bills, had her household effects appraised at a value of 10s. Her chattels included three trestles, two tables, one tablecloth, a pair of sheets, her wooden platters, a candlestick and some pewter and brass, obviously the simple furnishings of a widow. James Sprenger, a debtor who had fled the town, was a painter and mason. Amongst his goods, valued at 8s., were three stones of Chalk, four little stone pots, two graining stones, 'wone potte of yello Culler' and a little supply of mustard seed, a reminder that a house painter had then to make up his own paints.

Surrey suffered from the severe dislocation of the economy resulting from the heavy mortality in the Black Death in 1348 and further cutbacks in population from the plagues that followed in 1361-2, 1387 and 1396 and for most of the 15th century the demographic picture appears to be one of falling population or at best stagnation. With falling prices and rising costs lords were 'very unsure of what path to take and switched back and forth between farming out their manors and keeping them in hand, before finally moving over to wholesale leasing in the 1390s'. From the standpoint of the peasant the fall in population was on the whole favourable. As demesnes shrank in size, the work of customary tenants was commuted for money payments. The peasants' standard of living also improved as relatively higher real wages could be earned than formerly, so that the peasant could afford more meat and dairy products which earlier had been regarded as luxuries. More money could be spent on houses and furnishings.

ELINOVR RVMMIN,

The famous Ale-wife of *England*.

Written by Mr. *Skelton*, Poet Laureat to King

Henry the egiht.

When Skelton *wore the Lawrell Crowne,*
My Ale put all the Ale-wiues downe.

LONDON
Printed for *Samuel Rand* 1624.

36 *Elinour Rummin, the early 16th-century ale-house keeper of Leatherhead was celebrated in ballad for more than two centuries.*

7

Surrey as a Rural Workshop (1560-1640)

New Water-Powered Industries

In a letter to John Aubrey, the author of the first detailed history of Surrey, John Evelyn wrote in 1675 of the former and then existing industrial sites in the parish of Wotton, near Dorking, and its neighbourhood.

> Not far from my brother's house, upon the streams and ponds, since filled up and drained, stood formerly many powder mills erected by my ancestors who were the very first to bring that invention into England [Long Ditton to Godstone and Shere]. In this parish [of Wotton] were set up the first brass-mills for the casting, hammering into plates, cutting and drawing it into wire, that were in England ... but the mills are removed to a further distance from my brother's house. There was likewise a fulling mill upon the same stream, now demolished, but the hammer for iron remains. These I mention because I do not remember to have seen such variety of mills and works upon so narrow a brook and in so little a compass: these being mills for corn, cloth, brass, iron and powder, etc.

Evelyn's pride in his family achievements have preserved for posterity his vivid record of industry near Wotton. Yet much the same story could have been told for the length and breadth of Surrey between 1560 and 1640, for Surrey was then a great workshop of England.

Evelyn was writing of the Tillingbourne stream which flowed through his family estate from strong springs on the northern flanks of Leith Hill, on its course to join the river Wey. A remarkable growth in industry took place on this stream during the late 16th and early 17th centuries which created an archetypal rural workshop before the Industrial Revolution in Britain. Thereafter the stream acquired a new importance as a source of energy driving grain and textile mills, trip-hammers for iron, brass and wire-manufacture and for the making of gunpowder, saw-milling, paper manufacture and knife-grinding. Water-using industries also gravitated to the river, notably leather-tanning, and in addition to other economic uses to which the regulated river was put, the floating of meadows being a conspicuous example, ornamental canals, serpented streams, cascades and waterfalls were applied to garden layouts with the same skilful engineering techniques initially acquired in the industrial management of water.

At the heart of manipulating water for these various industrial 'projects' was the Evelyn family whose experience of the many related problems and

51

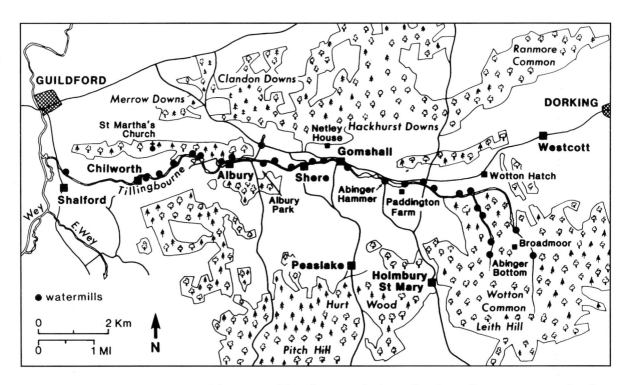

37 *Distribution of water-mills along the River Tillingbourne, 16th and 17th centuries.*

opportunities created by the practical application of water was to develop and diversify over the first four generations of the family residence at Wotton. The diarist's grandfather, George Evelyn (the first) who bought the Wotton estate in 1579 became famous as a manufacturer of gunpowder. His youngest son Richard, who succeeded to the Wotton inheritance in 1603, greatly extended and developed industry. As a 'thriving, neat, silent and methodical genius' he became involved in several different applications of water as well as having modern ideas on woodland conservation. He also had a remarkable practical knowledge of the soils and geology of his neighbourhood. Richard's rôle was followed, with less consistence, by his eldest son George (d.1699). John Evelyn's own tastes were towards re-afforestation and garden-making and these were to be his own special contribution to the changing landscape of the Tillingbourne valley, so repairing some of the damage done by woodland clearances which had been the price of industrialisation. Although the Evelyns were the most ambitious of the local projectors they were by no means the sole source of water-power technology in the Tillingbourne valley. The Hills of Abinger, the Morgans and Randalls of Chilworth, the Brays of Shere and the Lee-Steeres of Wotton and Ockley were also energetic participators in industrial ventures. Apart from the Lee-Steeres, the oldest landed family, the others, including the Evelyns, were *arriviste* Tudor gentry whose migration to the valley from Wales or the Welsh border with King Henry VII was evidently primarily due to the opportunities it offered to the enterprising industrialist.

Although the first new form of industrial activity brought into the Tillingbourne valley was that of iron manufacture, notably Thomas Elrington's forge at Abinger Hammer founded in 1557 (famous on account of its special exemption from restrictions on fuel-cutting within the area of London), gunpowder making became more important because it had better conditions of growth. The location and development of gunpowder manufacture was determined as much by a sufficiency of fuel supplies and of water power as by a sparsely populated countryside which offered greater safety in working. The sites were also accessible to London, then the chief source of imported saltpetre and of stores powder. Three early sites of gunpowder manufacture can be identified in the valley: near Wotton House, the Evelyn's family home; at Abinger (Elwix) mill downstream where the initial manufacturer of powder was probably Richard Hill, a previous lord of the manor of Abinger and a partner of George Evelyn I in powder-making; and at Chilworth where the East India Company was licensed in 1626 to make explosives for its own use. The Company disposed of its lease of the works ten years later when George Evelyn's patent was granted by the Crown to his competitors Samuel Cordwell and George Collins who erected new premises on the Chilworth site. When John Aubrey was compiling his history of Surrey (c.1675-80) there were 18 powder mills at Chilworth together with a boiling-corning-separating-and-finishing house, these strung out along the river to minimise explosion.

The brass industry initially provided products required for, or associated with, gunpowder. The earliest brass-making was associated with Thomas

38 Abinger Mill, *a landscape painting by William Mote, late 19th century.*

39 *George Scharf's* Limekilns *(c.1820) recalls a once familiar feature of the Surrey clay landscape.*

Steere of Wotton and Ockley who enticed hammermen, smiths and toolmakers to leave the sole then existing wire manufactory at Tintern in defiance of the monopoly of the Mineral and Battery Company. The monopolists, however, were successful defendants in a legal action which led to the closure of the Chilworth works in 1606. Steere had proposed to supply the London market with a wide range of consumer goods made from wire, including fine wire for weaving (a traditional local industry), and 'mouse traps, cages for birds, lattice-work for windows, buckles, chains, clasps for garments, fish-hooks, pack-needles, knitting-needles, rings for curtains' and other sundry items.

Richard Evelyn's infringement of the monopoly of the Mineral and Battery Company's brass-plate and wire-drawing operations was far more successful than Steere's. He set up brass and wire works on the site of Elwix mill, a former gunpowder mill and at Pigeon House Pond at Wotton House, possibly also the site of former powder-making. The Elwix mill by 1622 was a complex including a 'batter' mill (producing brass and copper plate for consumer goods such as pans, kettles, ladles, etc. (as well as the requirements of the powder industry), a wire-works and a copper mill which treated imported copper ingots with calamine stone to introduce zinc for making into brass.

Another important Surrey stream utilised to turn waterwheels was the Wandle, even though its watercourse was only nine miles long from its main source at Waddon, near Croydon, to where it entered the Thames at Wandsworth. From the first recorded history of this little stream, it has been put to work: at least 13 mills on its banks existed at Domesday. In 1610, 24 corn mills were grinding one-third of Surrey's corn supplied to London. In addition, several industrial works had developed. In 1571, for example, there is mention of a 'brazil' mill for grinding dyestuffs and fulling mills had been in operation since the 14th century. To overcome the small fall of 124 ft. and the tiny volume of the stream, the Wandle millers built pen-stocked ponds for the storage of water. In 1610 they successfully resisted a proposal to divert one-tenth of the precious Wandle water to London for domestic purposes. As early as 1589 some mills comprising two wheels 'under one roof' worked eight pairs of stones and were serviced by a wooden crane lifting corn from barges.

Ironmaking

The iron industry in Surrey was not so extensive as in Sussex and Kent. Nevertheless, it was an important activity in numerous parishes during the Middle Ages and during the period of exceptionally rapid growth in the 16th and early 17th centuries much of the iron ore was locally worked out. Until the late 15th century iron could only be produced in small quantities at a time in simple furnaces known as bloomeries. These were built on a circular floor or hearth made of sandstone, upon which alternate layers of charcoal and ore were placed in the form of a conical heap, the whole being covered by a thick layer of clay. Hand or foot bellows were inserted into the lowermost layers of charcoal and ore in order to provide the blast. The

40 *Surrey iron and glass manufacture (based on G.H. Kenyon,* The Wealden Glass Industry *[1967] and E. Straker,* Wealden Iron *[1931]). Townspeople kept glassworks and ironworks at a distance because of the local rise in the cost of fuel arising from these operations. Both Kingston-upon-Thames and Guildford successfully opposed these industries in the 16th and early 17th centuries.*

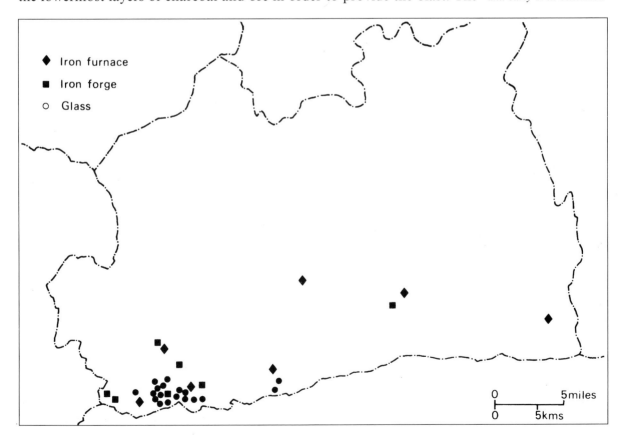

- ◆ Iron furnace
- ■ Iron forge
- ○ Glass

0 — 5 miles
0 — 5 kms

metal collected was a spongy or pasty mass called a 'bloom', and an outlet was made at the side of the hearth to permit the removal of slag or cinder. The blooms, weighing only about 50-150 lbs., were beaten into shape with hammers at a forge. From the early 15th century in Sussex such hammers were being worked by a large wheel turned by a stream of water, but no documentary evidence has yet been found for a similar development in Surrey. On the ground the visible evidence of a bloomery includes inconspicuous heaps of cinder and slag (less glassy and more 'nubbly' than that produced by the later blast furnaces), burnt clay, charcoal, and partially roasted ironstone. Such a bloomery furnace was being operated in 1354 at Tudeley in Newdigate and the mining of iron ore is mentioned at Horley Common in 1371, and on the estate of Christchurch, Canterbury in Charlwood in 1396. Very little other medieval documentary evidence has survived. It is the field archaeologist who will eventually fill in the details of medieval ironmaking; the recording of sites is far from complete in Surrey. Arduous fieldwork is required because most of the surviving bloomeries are hidden along stream banks or are protected by shaws and undergrowth from the plough.

In the late 15th and early 16th centuries the blast furnace was introduced from northern France to Surrey, in common with the rest of the Weald. Such furnaces were sited on relatively swift streams because their large bellows were operated by water power. Forges also used water-power hammers at this date. Streams were diverted into collecting points and waters were impounded by building earthen dams called 'bays' across the narrow valleys. On small brooks a succession of long, narrow ponds was needed as reservoirs. Many of these are now dry owing to the erosive power of a strong stream which has lowered their outlets. The 'hammer' or 'furnace' ponds that remain are amongst the most beautiful man-made features of the Weald.

Such furnaces consumed relatively large quantities of iron ore. In the west Surrey Weald around Haslemere the clay ironstone occurs at a constant horizon in a narrow, crescent-shaped belt below the Horsham stone which is the traditional roofing material in the district. The relict features of mining in the landscape are usually crater-like depressions on the ground surface between eight and 12 feet in diameter. These mark roughly infilled bell-pits, which were rarely more than 20 ft. deep. Well worked-over ground is pitted with so many water-filled hollows that it looks 'as if it has suffered a bombardment'.

The calling of 'Colyer', or charcoal-burner, necessitated his living near his fire in the woods, usually in a clearing. His methods of charcoal making remained unchanged for centuries. He gathered short lengths of oak into heaps six feet high built over a hearth. The wood was then covered with turf and ashes to limit the entrance of air. The heap was then fired at several points near the bottom and a draught of air induced by leaving a hole at the top. Later the hole was covered and when the flames penetrated the heap entirely the lower holes were closed.

Special interest attaches to the ironworks of Witley and Thursley heaths for detailed leases have survived which include inventories of the plant and tools in use. This supplies us with the best contemporary account of the various processes employed in a Wealden ironworks. These works are described in a lease of 1610 as being 'lately erected': in 1623 they were owned by Henry Bell from whom they passed to Anthony Smith. It is the latter's lease of the ironworks to William Yalden in 1666 which is so informative. The Thursley works then comprised a furnace where the ore was reduced and cast into sows or pigs. The forge (or hammer as it was usually called in Surrey) contained two fires called the 'finery' and the 'chafery'. The sows were first converted at the finery into short, thick blooms, and then into longer ones called 'anconies'. At the chafery the roughened ends of the anconies were founded off and made ready for market. At Smith's works at Thursley there was an upper and lower finery and one chafery.

Here and there it is still possible to recapture something of the atmosphere of the era of iron-working. To visit the site of the Ewood ironworks owned by Christopher Darrell, citizen and merchant tailor of London in the mid-16th century, one turns into an old track through still remote and extensive woodland in Newdigate parish which anciently formed part of Ewood Park and provided fuel for the furnaces and forges. Across the whole width of a natural hollow created by the river Mole runs a high and massive earthen embankment (bay) over a quarter of a mile long. This impounded 'a great pond' of 90 acres, the largest pond in Surrey until it was drained in the middle of the 19th century. A factory now occupies its site. The upper Mole, a mere brook in dry weather but turbulent and menacing after heavy rain, is tearing down and will soon breach the dam altogether if restoration is not soon completed. A delightful low half-timbered cottage, still called Ewood Mill, stands on the downstream of the bay. This was possibly the hammerman's house, but after the iron industry ended it was converted into a corn mill.

Glassmaking

Another important woodland industry in Elizabethan times was glassmaking. Unlike the more important and widespread charcoal iron industry, this was localised in the Surrey and Sussex Weald, south-west of Guildford. By 1560 the centre of the industry was in the Sussex parish of Wisborough Green, but Kirdford, Chiddingfold and Hambledon were also part of the 'core' manufacturing area. In this group of parishes there is evidence of glassmaking going back at least to the mid-14th century. In the late 16th century, the industry spread further to such parishes as Alfold and Ewhurst.

There is little trace of the glass industry in the present landscape. Excavated sites, usually in or near to coppice woodland, reveal merely a burnt patch and a few fragments of crucibles and glass. Only one glassmaking site has, however, been scientifically examined. It is at Blundell's Wood, Hambledon. This careful excavation tells us in some detail what a 14th-century 'glass house' was like. A wooden shed, roofed with tiles, probably covered the furnaces in which the glass was melted and annealed. Two primitive kilns, a large sub-rectangular one and a smaller 'beehive' type, lay on either side

41 *Medieval glass-maker.*

of a small, round oven and a working floor. E.S. Wood has suggested that the function of the main kiln was as a melting furnace and the smaller was for 'fritting' and annealing, whilst the small oven was probably for pre-heating pots. The pottery at this site is ascribed to *c*.1330.

The glassmakers were usually farmers using the local sands, ash and beech as a flux and oak billets to fuel the furnace. It was a craft handed down in families from generation to generation. The Peytrowes of Chiddingfold, and the Strudwicks of Kirdford were, for example, long-established glaziers. The surnames *Vitrearius* or *le Verir* occurring in 14th-century tax subsidies also probably record early practising glassmakers.

42 *The successive stages in the production of glass in the late 16th century.*

The rapid expansion of this historic industry in the reign of Elizabeth I is associated with improved methods of making window glass introduced from the Continent by immigrant craftsmen. A number of French families are recorded in the local parish registers. The most famous amongst them is John Carré of Arras who set up as glassmaker at Fernfold *c*.1567 to make 'Normandy and Lorraine' glass and who was buried at Alfold in 1572. Another of the Lorrainers and Normans in Surrey was Isaac Bungar (died 1643). His father probably came from France with Carré as one of those who taught Surrey folk how to make good quality window glass, then in huge demand in the fury of great rebuilding after the Reformation. Bungar is described in 1614 as 'gentleman' and owner of glass furnaces in Surrey and Sussex. He bought considerable woodland to secure fuel for his furnaces and came to monopolise production, but could not produce enough glass to satisfy the demand owing to the high cost of fuel in Surrey, forced up by the insatiable needs of glass- and iron-makers and by farmers who were beginning to use lime-kilns. He then faced, and lost, his first critical battle. A coal-fired glassmaking process was perfected by Sir Robert Mansell in Staffordshire, who enforced his monopoly of making glass in this new way so successfully that Isaac Bungar closed down his last wood-fired furnace in the Weald in 1618, after a fierce struggle. This marks the effective end of the forest glass industry in Surrey. Its most remarkable memorials are the small windows of Chiddingfold and Kirdford churches glazed with fragments of the old locally-made window glass, including many coloured pieces, which Cooper, and Hugh Kenyon, who earlier worked with Winbolt, have reconstructed.

Clothmaking

For more than 400 years from the 13th to the 17th centuries, clothmaking was one of the staple industries of Surrey. Its former widespread distinction within the county can be pieced together from the cumulative evidence which can be drawn from probate inventories, tax lists and various deeds. Almost every Surrey village had inhabitants engaged in one or more stages in the production of woollen cloth. Caterham, Nutfield and West Horsley, by way of examples, had each their shearmen and weavers in the early 17th century. Places which by then had decayed as centres of woollen manufacture can be identified with the aid of place-names. The 'Great Teynter Field' at Kingston-upon-Thames, mentioned in a document of 1699 for instance, perpetuates the open space where the citizens laid out their cloth on racks (tenterhooks) to dry. The decline of the industry at Kingston is doubtless connected with the very limited water-power available from the Hogsmill Brook. At neighbouring Mitcham, on the Wandle, the village was still busily engaged in whiting and bleaching and other finishing processes, but as the 17th century advanced Mitcham steadily abandoned the manufacture of woollen cloth for the new calico industry which throve with the rising demand for costly fabrics from wealthy London residents. The villages of Gomshall and Shere were outstanding as weaving centres. In 1380 they had between them 14 weavers and 42 spinners besides pelterers, shearers, dyers, fullers and so on. Drapers were mentioned in Shere and Gomshall and neighbouring villages in 1436 and in Henry VIII's reign Shere is mentioned in a list of places at which long cloths of 20, 22 and 24 yards were made. The houses of clothmakers, together with individual farmhouses and houses of village craftsmen, such as blacksmiths and wheelwrights, some of whom were also yeomen and husbandmen, explain the present character of Shere village.

More and more the woollen cloth trade shrank in 17th-century Surrey to the towns and villages of the south-west on the fast-flowing river Wey or its

43 *Spinning wheel (after Gertrude Jekyll).*

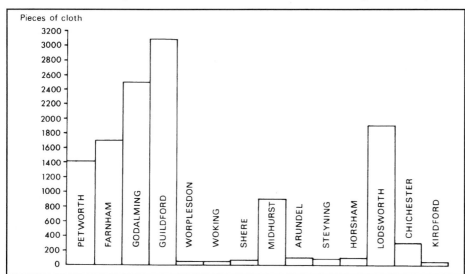

44 *Guildford cloth manufacture. Data based on original ulnage returns in the Guildford Muniment Room (Loseley Ms.). The production shown represents the position in the 1570s.*

45 *Crossways Farm, Abinger, a good example of a brick-fronted small house of the early 17th century, a home of a wool merchant.*

46 *This tool for cutting heath-turf was used traditionally to gather fuel by poor cottagers in areas where woodland had been devastated for industrial purposes. The operator threw the whole weight of his body against the heavy cross-handle.*

many tumbling tributaries, to Farnham, Guildford, Godalming, and their outlying villages such as Ash, Shere, Stoke and Wonersh. Both Godalming and Guildford possess coats of arms bearing wool-packs. Many a Surrey yeoman acquired wealth and gentility from wool or cloth, and this social enhancement was expressed in domestic architecture. The most celebrated example of this kind is Crossways Farm, Abinger, the brick-fronted home of a 17th-century wool merchant. Where the cloth industry was important the houses are often distinguished by their comparatively large first-floor windows which lighted the loom, or wide overhanging upper rooms which provided additional space for weaving. Yet another building device was a central balconied room set aside for weaving as at Shere and Wonersh.

Much new building and re-building went on between 1580 and 1640, based largely on the prosperity of clothmaking, so that there are many timber-framed houses, of which at least eight at Shere were built originally as open halls.

Papermaking

As the cloth industry in Surrey collapsed into dereliction with the rise of new fabrics and the growing competition from more favoured centres in England drawing upon imported wools, the old fulling mills were increasingly bought up by London paper manufacturers. In the reign of James I Surrey was the leading centre in England for the manufacture of coarse brown paper used in packaging. By the end of the 17th century Surrey was also producing high-grade paper on a considerable scale. In John Evelyn's account of his visit to Byfleet paper mills in 1678 he mentions the linen being torn to shreds by pestles operated by water-power before being converted to high quality paper, and also the same operation on woollen rags destined for cheaper paper. In the finishing stage the paper was suspended on wire-trays locally produced by wire-drawing mills, themselves suffering severe competition by the end of the century from Black Country producers. By this time Godalming had become the leading Surrey paper centre.

The Exploitation of Woodland

The most lasting effects of early industry in the Tillingbourne valley and elsewhere in Surrey were on the woodland. In general, the wood-using indus-tries in the 16th and early 17th centuries, although initially destroying wood-land, had in the end an opposite effect by providing a market for the regular cutting of coppices for charcoal. Nevertheless, despite the woodland man-agement which tended to prevail on privately-owned woods, an exploitative strategy was deployed on commonlands. In the Tillingbourne valley and on the Lower Greensand further south west, the commons were so extensive that the progressive depletion of their tree cover for industry profoundly altered the visual aspect of the countryside. The wood scarcity had also deleterious social effects, for the poorer classes were obliged to seek alterna-tive domestic fuels such as turf, peat, furze, heather and bracken. In broad terms the landscape on the poorer soils of the Tillingbourne valley was transformed by 16th- and 17th-century industry from once virtually continu-ous woodland to that of a series of self-protected 'islands' of systematic encoppicing and plantations in a sea of newly-created heathland on which the continual impact of fuel-cutting virtually prevented tree regeneration.

The depletion of the wood cover and the change from wood-getting to turf-cutting amongst smallholders and cottagers in the cloth-making villages such as Wonersh, Bramley, Gomshall and Shere can be illustrated by the history of the Churt (now called Hurtmore or the Hurtwood). Although it was improbably continuously wooded in the later Middle Ages this extensive area was invariably described as a common wood (*boscus* or *silva*). In 1454 the cutting of wood was still supervised by annually-appointed wood reeves who confirmed that all tenants of the manor were entitled to wood and fuel at the rate of seven wagon loads for larger farmers down to three cartloads for smallholders. But an important change in vegetation is indicated by the prohibition of cutting wood on the common, first promulgated in 1582 and by the term waste (*vastum*) for the Churt in 17th-century documents.

In 1654 attempts were made to regularise the cutting of heath (*brueria*), but so general and damaging did the practice of fern-cutting for barns and brick-making and lime-burning and that of turves and furze for domestic fuel become that a group of leading tenants covenanted in 1708 to defend their rights against the illicit cutting of heath on the east side of the Churt. By this date all the evidence is that the remnants of the old woodland had virtually perished.

8

The Improvers (1560-1640)

Much of the rebuilding of Surrey between 1560 and 1640 was due to the expansion of agriculture into medieval forests, parks and other marginal lands previously turned to limited account. The rising population of both town and countryside, which increased the demand for food and consequently for land, was responsible for this development. The rapid growth of London had a particularly marked effect on land use in Surrey, it now being within the ambit of the metropolitan food market.

Old estate maps and detailed leases enable one to reconstruct at a local level a picture of the changing face of Surrey at this period. By way of a single example, we can trace something of the successive stages of land improvement and new buildings at Portnall Park in Egham, one of the numerous similar projects in Surrey at the time. This was the work of several generations of a yeoman family who cherished their hard-won surroundings and tried to make them habitable at the expense of that terrible antagonist, the Bagshot Sands. The Park was originally part of the Royal Forest of Windsor. It was disparked before 1566 when Viscount Montague, the grandson of Sir Anthony Browne, a courtier and office-holder under Henry VIII, sold it to his yeoman tenant, Henry Lane of Coworth in the adjoining parish of Old Windsor. Lane had difficulty in raising the full purchase price of £200, an event his descendants doubtless recalled when they examined their rising rent rolls and travelled over their steadily improving estate. It was Lane's son-in-law and grandson who were the main 'improvers' of Portnall, and three new tenements carved out of the Park come to our notice. 'Old House Farm' of 200 acres was originally taken in hand by Lane and his heirs. About 1646 the farmhouse was rebuilt, and in 1656 and again in 1678 the farm was let for periods of 20 years at rents of £32 and £40 per annum respectively. Clearly this was a steadily improving property of changing aspect, but the comparatively low rentals suggest that much of the acreage remained poor grazing. A second parcel of the Park, called 'New Grounds' and covering 140 acres, began its first stage of reclamation when a new farmhouse and barns were built about 1632. This poor, heathy ground was first let for an annual rent of £15, but in 1635 this was abated to £13 10s., and in 1646 reduced again to £13. The rapid turnover of tenants and the very low and falling rent suggests that much of this farm was still only profitable as a rabbit warren. A third portion of the Park was let as a smallholding of 12 acres. The tenant was required to move the existing barn to a more convenient place and to modernise and enlarge the house by adding a brick chimney and two 'fire-rooms', i.e. chambers with fireplaces. This little tenement was let at £3 per annum before these improvements and at £6 afterwards. Thus even the modest land improvement at Portnall involved the rebuilding of two farm-houses and the modernising of a third. It is a story of the demand of the farmer for a more elaborate homestead that could be repeated over the length and breadth of Surrey.

The Portnall leases also give us an insight into contemporary techniques of land reclamation. The tenants were expected to 'devonshire' (denshire) the heaths, that is steadily to take into cultivation by paring the bracken and furze and ploughing in ashes after burning in the manner long prac-tised in Devon. This involved the maintenance of a lime kiln. The landlord ensured that tenants carefully preserved thorn trees, withies and selected birch trees needed for new fences but encouraged the felling of other trees to make way for crops. Birch, the most prolifically-growing tree in the Forest, provided most of the timber used on local farms and tenants were required to lop it 'as accustomedly hath been used, and not to be cut down to the ground, but to be cut in good husbandlike manner, that it may grow again'. Beech trees specifically set aside as *playsers* for providing branches used for plashing (the laying of stock fences by planting living stems or 'pleachers') were to be left unlopped.

Towards the end of Elizabeth's reign, marked changes in domestic archi-tecture, representing a surge forward in comfort, became apparent in Sur-rey, as in most of England. The wealthy learned the cosiness of tapestried and oak-panelled rooms and the joy of a wide six-light window through which the sun poured in to flood the entire room. A staircase became a stately feature providing an easy access to rooms newly built over the medieval open hall, an improvement made possible by collecting smoke that had formerly escaped through the rafters and gablets of the hall by smoke bays or smoke hoods. With increasing prosperity there was also a desire to enlarge the house, normally achieved by demolishing two end bays and building a cross wing which then provided the best living rooms. In the early 17th century bricks became readily available and smoke-bay hearths were lined with brick and a brick chimney built with a bacon-curing chamber on one side of it.

Surrey possesses some of the finest examples of old brick, half-timbered cottages that it is possible to find in any English county. Even within a mile of the perimeter of Gatwick airport, amidst some of the most drastic land-scape changes, are more than a score of 15th- and 16th-century houses, some heavily disguised in 18th-century or even modern fronts upon the vast strength of their native oak beams. In the parish of West Horsley there are half a dozen half-timbered houses along The Street and another cluster of yeomen's farmsteads further afield.

Even at Charlwood in the deep Surrey Weald, the modernisation of Pixton's was as early as 1571 and new houses with chimneys were being

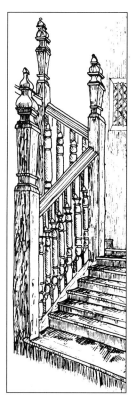

47 *Typical early 17th-century newel staircase, Shoelands, Puttenham (after* Victoria County History).

built by the end of Elizabeth's reign, such as Charlwood Place Farm. Numerous yeomen's houses renovated before 1600 were not provided with a chimney stack, presumably on account of expense, but with a specially constructed smoke-bay. One of the finest and best-known examples of a 15th-century house altered in the 16th and 17th centuries is Unstead Manor House, Bramley. The earliest surviving parts are an open hall house of about 1400. The hall formerly extended farther to the right. The door and carved lintel are probably original. The lovely crown-post roof and soot-blackened rafters indicate that the hall was formerly open to the roof. The centre crown-post was moulded and carved with some care by a medieval carpenter, because it would have been the main decorative feature in the centre of the open roof of the house. The cross-wing at Unstead was added about 1600 on the site of one room of the medieval house. The struts and braces in its upper part served a decorative as well as a structural purpose. Its fireplaces were carved in a form of hard Chalk.

Another fine half-timbered house illustrating the great social changes taking place in 16th- and 17th-century Surrey is Nurscombe in Bramley. A cross-wing was added to the medieval hall house, the hall was floored over, and a chimney added *c.*1620 to provide a 'great parlour'. This turned it into a comfortable yeoman's farmstead with a dairy, buttery, wash and brew house, all of which services were originally provided by the medieval kitchen.

The village of Shere is one of the most rewarding places to study Tudor and Stuart domestic buildings because of the prosperity of the cloth trade which has already been noted (p.59). Old Cottage in Upper Street was originally built as a timber-framed open-hall house about 1580-1620 but a

48 *Typical of the re-fronted houses in Surrey of the Georgian period is the fine town house at Limpsfield. The side elevation and exterior brick chimney tell of its extreme antiquity.*

V *John Norden's map of the Royal Forest of Windsor (1607). The Surrey bailiwick brought local farmers into close touch with the Crown. Elizabeth I exempted the men of Pirbright from the obligation of providing provender for the royal horses in compensation for damage done to crops by deer. James I, a keen hunstman, threatened to prohibit swine-grazing in the Forest unless holes dug by rootling pigs were regularly filled in.*

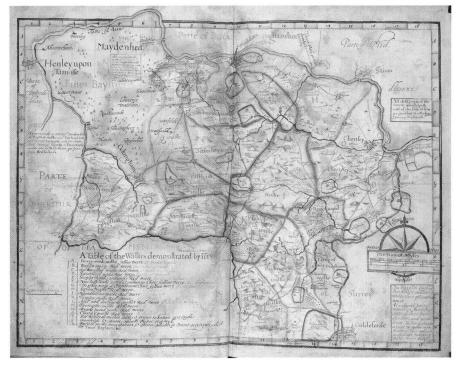

VI *The Claremont Landscape Garden initiated by Vanbrugh. William Kent made Bridgeman's design less formal from 1729 and in Horace Walpole's famous phrase 'leaped the fence and saw that all nature was a garden' by creating the ha-ha along the edge of the re-modelled garden.*

VII *George Scharf's* Acre Lane, Brixton *(1820) captures the now roaring City street when it was still a rustic world inhabited by cowkeepers, nurserymen and smallholders, and visited by strolling London families refreshing themselves on Sundays.*

VIII *Richard Redgrave's* The Emigrants' Last Sight of Home *(1858) depicts a carpenter's family leaving the beautiful but desperately poor parish of Abinger for a new country. Earlier Charles Barclay, of Bury Hill, had assisted in the emigration of more than eighty persons from the Dorking district.*

chimney was inserted soon afterwards. Tudor Cottage in the same street has a similar history and was occupied by weavers as late as the 18th century. There are many more delightful old buildings in Upper Street but the Post Office Stores, Bank Terrace and Woodbine Cottages in Middle Street are the most significant. At the south end are the remains of an early 15th-century house with a crown post roof and cross wing. The middle part (the Post Office) was probably built in the mid-16th century with a chimney and continuous jetty along the front to replace an earlier open-hall house. The northern cross wing was built early in the 17th century. This has a well-panelled parlour almost certainly built by John Stonell, a fustian weaver, who used the ground floor in this wing for his weaving.

49 *Polesden Lacey, the old house, built 1631-2 and demolished c. 1818.*

Another great embellishment to the present Surrey scene was created by one of the most characteristic forms of rural settlement in Surrey, the mill hamlet. This is a typical 16th- and 17th-century addition to the pattern of rural settlement directly due to the spread of industry into the countryside with its general increase in employment either in industry itself or the related woodland activities. This type of new settlement is particularly notable in the Tillingbourne valley: Broadmoor and Friday Street in Wotton; Abinger Bottom, Abinger Hammer and Sutton in Abinger; Sutton and Pitland Street (now part of Holmbury St Mary); Chilworth in St Martha's. Other older centres were expanding with milling, notably Weston in Albury. Each is built in the dominant architectural style of the early 17th century which in central Surrey normally took the form of half-timbered 'mud' dwellings, subsequently brick-nogged, but also occasionally of stone buildings. From documentary sources it is sometimes possible to date fairly precisely the origin of these mill-hamlets. Thus Abinger Bottom is described as 'six newly erected cottages', enclosures and a mill (at Friday Street) in 1607.

Moving up the social scale the houses built or enlarged by the ironmasters greatly embellish the present Surrey scene. The ironmasters were generally accounted members of the local gentry and their houses equalled, or surpassed, contemporary manor houses. One was 'Rake', the house owned by Bell and Smith, who were the Thursley ironmasters. This is a good specimen of an Elizabethan house. It has a panelled parlour containing a very delicately carved oak mantelpiece bearing the initials H.B. (for Henry Bell), and the date 1602, but its most important structural feature is the staircase which is evidently a transition between the earliest stairs winding round a newel or within solid walls and the later and more practical one of a square plan with newels and balustrades. Another house greatly improved by a flourishing ironmaster was 'Burningfold' in Dunsfold, the home of Richard Marche, owner of Dunsfold furnace at the end of the 16th century. Its nucleus was a medieval hall house with the standard open hall, offices and solar, or sleeping room. Marche provided a fine new front, of a design similar to that of nearby Tangley Manor and dated 1582, and inserted rooms into the first floor, served by a plain winding newel oak staircase.

Turning now to gentlemen's mansions, one of the earliest and most exquisite achievements was Sutton Place, built by Sir Richard Weston, an intimate member of Henry VIII's court, *c.*1523-5. The design was probably influenced by the châteaux Weston had observed on his travels on the king's business in the country of the Loire, then the centre of artistic life in France. Sutton Place is built in brick and terra-cotta around a quadrangle enclosing a space of 81ft. on each side and fronted by an arched gateway and flanked by lofty hexagonal towers. It survives as one of the best examples of an early type of country house of the Surrey landed gentleman.

A new development in Surrey is marked by Loseley, built in 1561-9 by Sir William More. This was the first Surrey mansion laid out on an H- or E-shaped plan which set the fashion for two generations and more, and is characteristic of Elizabethan domestic architecture in both Surrey and Sussex. The north wing of the house containing the main appartments still survives.

It is instructive to examine an inventory of the contents of a gentleman's house in Elizabeth's reign. It relates to Beddington Manor, the home of Sir Francis Carew. The furniture in the parlour, the main living room, included new luxuries such as Turkish and Venetian carpets and no less than 18 paintings, but it was sparsely and rather uncomfortably furnished. Ten 'joyned stoulles' and two leather chairs, one long table and one small table completed the main living room furniture. The 'great chamber', or main bedroom, contained only the bedstead, a chair in satin and a 'great wenscote cheast' and, although the bed hangings were richly woven and embroidered, there is still little variety in furniture.

50 Nonsuch Palace was built in 1538 on the site of the older village of Cuddington, near Ewell, by command of Henry VIII. The palace passed in and out of royal control in the 16th century. Charles II granted it to his mistress, the Duchess of Cleveland who, from 1682 onwards, had the house demolished and materials sold. The park was divided into farms. Little remains today of the Palace but a few earthworks.

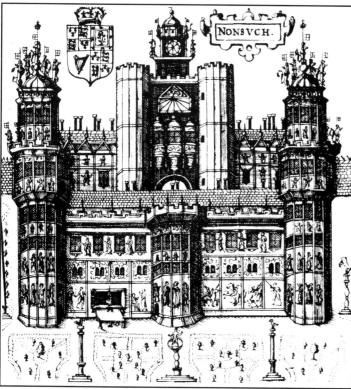

The small farmer continued to live frugally, as is suggested by the inventory of goods of John Potter, a farmer of Thorpe who died in 1637. His primary implements were a horse-drawn plough and a pair of harrows and his dung-cart. A flitch of bacon was in store and three sows, two hogs, two yearling bullocks and two calves and 18 acres under corn constituted his only wealth. His house comprised hall, kitchen and chamber with loft above. In the hall were merely a cupboard (perhaps under the stairs), one long table, a chair, a stool and a form, evidently for himself, his wife and his children respectively. In his kitchen was the traditional fireplace with its brass pots, kettles, fire shovel, pair of tongs, pot-hanger, spit and grid-iron. The bedstead and two chests were the only furnishings in the chamber, and the loft contained 'bedsteadles', bunks for the children.

Changing South London

The local community engaged in Surrey agriculture and industry was far more subject to natural and civil catastrophe than it is today. Bermondsey in the 16th and 17th centuries was particularly prone to epidemics, presumably on account of its congested streets and proximity to London. Between 1555 and 1608 heavy mortality occurred on three occasions—in September and October 1563 (169 burials in the parish churchyard), August and September 1593 (150 burials), and in the terrible catastrophe of July to September 1603 when 500 inhabitants died. These death rolls, compiled from the extant parish registers, are to be compared with an average of 20-25 burials each month. The epidemic of 1603 took off scores of children and adolescents as also did a less severe outbreak in 1608: diphtheria or scarlet fever may have been responsible. Paupers were also particularly vulnerable to disease, but the healthy and strong of each generation were clearly cut back repeatedly by epidemics. In the countryside the incidence of plague and other epidemics was less severe but still virulent. The Dorking parish registers reveal comparatively large death rolls in 1563, 1593, 1603 and 1610, and those of Charlwood, a Wealden parish, tell much the same story. Nineteen persons died here of plague in less than three months in 1610, and several families suffered severely. Mortlake escaped the epidemic disease of 1603 and 1610 but suffered dreadfully from the plague of 1665, 205 of the villagers dying in that year, 65 in the month of September alone.

Standing apart as a community of its own was Southwark, cut off from the main body of the metropolis save for London Bridge, used by craftsmen when visiting their guildhalls. By the early 17th-century Southwark was well established as a home of immigrants. Since the 16th century, refugees from Flanders, Holland and France, exiled for their religious beliefs, had settled there, bringing their independence, ideals and skills and turning Southwark into a centre of the weaving and stone-cutting industry and religious nonconformity. On the river front were the wharves, coal and timber yards. Behind these along Gravel Lane, Love Lane, Angel Lane, Dirty Lane, Orange Street, Lemon Street and Melancholy Lane were the cloth factories, glass houses and stonemasons' yards that employed the local inhabitants.

With its weaker local government than London itself and medieval rights of sanctuary enjoyed in the liberties of Paris Gardens and the Clink, a long standing reputation was gained from its notorious stews. Numerous inns, some with galleries which were the forerunners of the Elizabethan theatre, lined the Borough and other streets leading to London Bridge, alternating with bear gardens, bull-baiting rings and bowling alleys. Queen Elizabeth attended bear and bull baiting here as did Pepys after the 'sport' had been restored by Charles II. In these dubious surroundings actors, expelled from Puritan-controlled London in 1575, swarmed here including Shakespeare and Beaumont and Fletcher, Shakespeare having a house at the *Boar's Head* opposite the church of St Mary Overie amidst theatres including the Rose, founded *c.*1587, the Swan and Globe in 1599.

51 This 16th-century plan of Bankside depicts (on the left) part of the manor of Paris Gardens, Southwark; part of the land of the Bishop of Winchester; the Falcon Inn, *from whence coaches went to all parts of Kent, Surrey and Sussex; theatres for bull- and bear-baiting; pike ponds, for storing the royal fish; and other places of amusement. The district lay near the south end of the present Blackfriars bridge.*

Nearby several villages were scattered along the Thames. Lambeth, dominated by Lambeth Palace, with its extensive garden and park, and the houses of the bishops of Rochester and Carlisle, dukes of Norfolk and other wealthy men, was particularly prestigious and fashionable. Further south, Camberwell and Peckham were small villages and Dulwich consisted of little more than the college, founded in the early 17th century by the former owner of the Rose Theatre in Southwark. Putney, the birthplace of Thomas Cromwell, was another village surrounded by open fields which was so changed by 1656 that the inhabitants petitioned Oliver Cromwell to pave its long and broad high street. Streatham was a 'small, scattering village' at the end of the 17th century which had become a popular residential area, enhanced by the discovery of the Spa Well in 1660. Croydon was also growing around the newly-built market house in 1566.

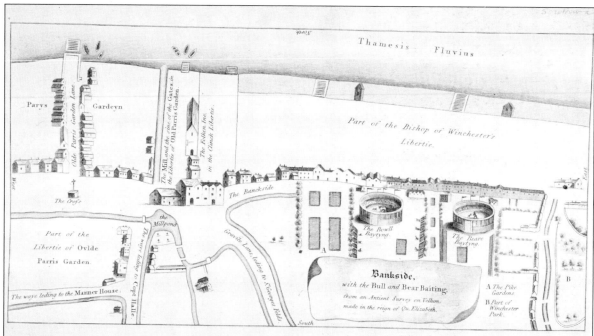

9

The Age of Luxury (1640-1740)

After the Restoration in 1660 and still more so from the Revolution in 1688, the wealth of England notably increased. Under these influences London extended more than at any time in its previous history, foreshadowing everything that was to come. As early as 1629 the artist-ambassador Rubens had marvelled at the size and grandeur of London's 'outward cincture'. It was from Inigo Jones that wealthy Londoners derived their avid taste for continental architecture, landscape design, painting and sculpture. A distinctive characteristic of this development was the beauty of country houses on the rural margins of London. Travelling from the coast on the old Lewes road in the 1720s, one would have encountered the first houses of London citizens at Carshalton; fine large mansions, looking more like the seats of the nobility rather than country houses of citizens and merchants. From the wooded hillside of still rural Mitcham, the hayfields of Clapham, Streatham and Tooting could be seen similarly invaded by large mansions. From the rising ground of Clapham the view eastwards took in the market gardens and fields of Camberwell and Peckham, containing some of the finest houses outside London itself, and westwards, towards Coombe and Kingston (fig.60), the wooded country was similarly bespangled with new buildings. Camberwell and other villages near London were, in fact, shedding their old half-timbered houses for handsome modern ones in brick, built to high standards of quality and design. As early as 1661 a lease of land stipulated that in place of an 'old ruinous messuage' fronting on the road at Camberwell church was to be built a brick house with 'fire chimneys' on well constructed foundations and with a ceiling height of eight feet for the principal rooms. The house was to be set back in the orchard of the old house and a brick wall constructed to embellish it. The specification for this dwelling epitomises the architectural change in domestic building which was to transform the entire face of Surrey on the fringe of London, bringing with it periwigged and be-powdered citizens into Surrey's countryside.

The finest houses of all, more like palaces than houses, had begun to line the Thames between Chelsea and Weybridge. 'England never had such a glorious show to make in the world before', wrote Defoe. Horace Walpole, who hated country life, lamented this rural extension of London into Surrey and Middlesex. 'Think what London would be if the chief houses were in

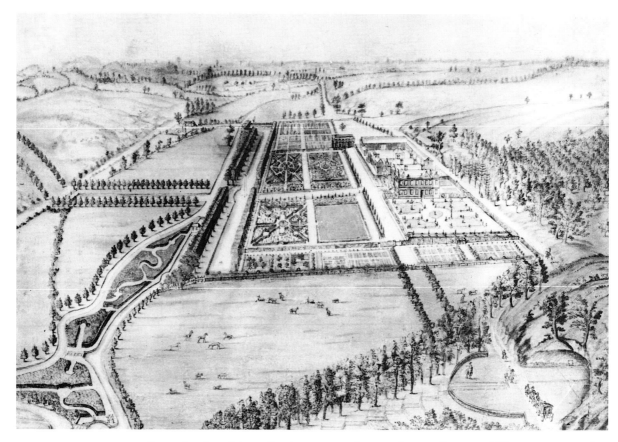

52 *Moor Park, Farn-ham, c.1690, the home of the highly accomplished Sir William Temple. In his retirement he indulged in gardening, a lifelong passion and completed his essay* Of Gardens. *He created at Moor Park an earthly paradise accor-ding to the notion of his day with parterres, long terraces, retaining walls, formal canals, pleached alleys and gazebos.*

it, as in the cities of other countries, and not dispersed like a great rarity of plums in a vast pudding of country'. This fury of building is one of the earliest manifestations of that deeply-rooted British preference for country life which distinguished London from continental cities such as Amster-dam, Paris, Bologna and Florence, and was destined to reshape Surrey landscape and its society. The *nouveaux riches* craved for a country house in which to spend the summer months (the roads were too miry in winter to a make a permanent residence feasible), 'to draw their breath in a clean aire' before returning for the winter to the 'Smoke and Dirt, Sin and Seacoal' of the busy city.

The Thames-side house at Ham deserves special recognition for it re-mains alone in Surrey as a 17th-century house with contents that have survived to a remarkable degree intact. Entering Ham House one savours to the full the atmosphere and spirit of the late 17th century. Its rooms are small, in the fashion of the time, but are lavishly furnished (in great contrast to the plainness of even an important room of an Elizabethan house) with profuse French-style furniture and all sorts of original hangings—velvet, brocade, damask—fringed with silk in silver and gold. Nothing is so vividly expressive of the 'politer but ruinously expensive way of life' introduced into Surrey after the Restoration than the remarkable survival of Ham House.

53 *The Long Gallery, Ham House, brought to a high point of furnishing. In the 18th century it was thought a perfect model of a mansion of the previous century, Horace Walpole considering that 'you could think yourself a hundred miles off and a hundred years back'.*

54 *A parterre of box, santolina and lavender at Ham House, restored on the basis of a 1671 plan of the garden. In the background is a sweeping brick wall decorated with the plaster-casts of the busts of Roman emperors. The visitor now sees 'a lordly house from one of the best periods of English architecture with a garden to match'.*

55   *Detail from William Schellinks'* Epsom Common and Wells, *1662. The scene shown was three-quarters of a mile west of Epsom village. A small building houses the Wells and people can be seen taking the waters behind the railings. Note the horse-riding, the chief recreation.*

56   *The Vauxhall Gardens showing the Grand Walk and an orchestra playing. So popular were the gardens that patrons' carriages caused traffic jams.*

57 J. Esselens' view of Kingston-upon-Thames from Coombe Hill, c.1650. The Surrey Hills are in the distance. Hampton Court Palace is shown on the extreme right.

All this was the work of Elizabeth Dysart and her second husband, created Duke of Lauderdale in 1672, a powerful member of the CABAL ministry. They extended and modernised the house built in 1610 and furnished it with luxuries remarkable even in that lavish age to match their ambitious rôle in Restoration political and social life. They bounded the grounds with a canal leading into the Thames by a water-gate, as in the manner of the perfect French villas on the river Loire or the style of Dutch patricians' houses on the river Vecht, and laid out a formal garden in the French mode with a parterre extending to a square lawn divided by side gravel paths which led to a 'wilderness' on a cart-wheel plan. In all but detail the garden (though not the canal which also deserves re-creation) has survived and has been restored by the National Trust according to an original plan of 1670 still hanging in the house. The garden is now again like 'a matching saucer to a beautiful cup'.

It was in the 17th century that the North Downs first acquired a reputation as a health resort and place of recreation. Banstead's medical fame was evidently brief for by Aubrey's day London physicians no longer prescribed its 'wholesome air', preferring to send patients to the neighbouring spa at Epsom, or to Cotmandean, near Dorking, where Defoe noted that 'some learned physicians have singled out as the best air in England'. Banstead and its downland, however, continued to hold the affections of wealthy London families as a sporting centre. John Tolland (1711) regarded its downs as the finest in the world, 'being covered with grass finer than Persian carpets and perfumed with wild thyme and juniper'. This mat of soft, springy grass was admirable for riding, hunting, shooting and horse-racing, all sports practised with ever-growing indulgence by leisure-lovers in post-Restoration London. Banstead and Epsom became the acknowledged Cockney paradise. Both had racecourses and abundant facilities for physical exercise.

Epsom's chief claim to fame was a spa. Its heyday was brief. The origins of Epsom Spa can be traced to the early 17th century, but it does not appear to have become popular until after the Restoration, when the age was more completely identified with pleasure. Pepys, Dorothy Osborne and Celia Fiennes and many others have recorded their impressions. For the appearance of this infant spa, we can draw upon an excellent engraving by William Schellinks (drawn 1662) (fig.55). Apparently, Epsom was still primarily a medical centre with few facilities for taking the waters; what little was available in the way of social facilities was in the village, a quarter of a mile away. Tolland tells us in 1711 that the old wells on Epsom Common (depicted in Schellinks' drawing) were then less regarded than new wells established on the western edge of Epsom itself. In the meantime, a reception room had been built at the old wells; this was demolished in 1804, by which time Epsom had long since ceased to be a spa. Tolland gives an admirable account of the new wells and the growing town of Epsom which had sprung up around them. It appears to have been a veritable 'garden-city'. Tastefully ornamented houses spread along a tree-lined avenue shaped in the form of a crescent, a mile in length. Many houses had arbours of clipped yew or box and under these the summer residents took their ease with 'a cheerful glass and a pipe'. Epsom Spa was clearly no more a part of Surrey than Brighton was to become part of Sussex. 'By the conversation of those who walk here', added Tolland, 'you would fancy yourself on the Exchange at St James', or in an East India factory, or with the army in Flanders.' Here Whig and Tory patrons ignored their political prejudices and joined fraternally in gossip. Bowling greens provided recreation in the mornings. An orchestra played in the afternoons, and a ball was held most evenings. Above the town was the Ring, a high part of the Downs where on Sunday evenings as many as 60 coaches would gather for the sake of the view.

All this luxury was generating handicrafts, industry and population on the south bank of the Thames. John Rocque's detailed *Survey of London* (1746) shows the maze of alleys, yards and tenements and the closely-built houses. Some large foundations had come into existence such as St Thomas's (rebuilt as a hospital in 1701-6) and Guy's opened in 1725 as a hospital for incurables. More wharves and timber yards stretched along the Thames towards Westminster Bridge (shown on Rocque's map but not actually opened until 1750) but then gave way to open fields and gardens past Lambeth Palace and the Horse ferry (later replaced by Lambeth Bridge) as the ornamental lighting and fashionable walks of Vauxhall Spring Gardens were approached. Lambeth Marsh was an area of open fields, pasture and haunt for game before its enclosure in 1806 to facilitate the building of roads for the new Waterloo Bridge.

Many waterside districts were notorious for their squalor and poverty. Defoe writes of the 'loathsome ditches' between Lambeth and Rotherhithe and St George's Fields:

These filthy places receive all the sinks, necessary houses and drains from dye houses, wash houses, fell mongers, slaughter houses and all kinds of offensive trades; they are continually full of carrion and the most odious of all offensive stench proceeds from them... the terror even of the inhabitants themselves ... notorious fountains of stench, enough to corrupt the very air and make the people sick and faint as they pass by ...

By this time Surrey had become famous for its gardens and landscaped parks. The new art form of the Renaissance garden is best seen at Hampton Court but its creator, Henry VIII, developed similar, if smaller, retreat gardens at Nonsuch and Oatlands. These Tudor gardens were the product of stylistic communication with France, including Francis I's Fontainebleau, which, in turn, responded to the aesthetic impulses from Renaissance Italy. Examples of courtiers' mansions and gardens strongly influenced by the same movement include Richard Weston's at Sutton Place. The reign of James I had been marked by a new impetus in garden design attributable to the arrival in England of Solomon de Caux, a French hydraulic engineer. A Renaissance style was given to Richmond Palace by means of elaborate fountains and grottoes, and a more rigid geometry of parterres and avenues, replacing more haphazard medieval arrangements by a design conceived as a whole and architecturally related to the house. A still further Italianate advance was taken by the first 'English Palladio', Inigo Jones, in the 1630s. He inspired gardens such as those at Wimbledon House, owned by the Cecils, Ham House, and a modernised Oatlands, home of Queen Henrietta Maria, which was gardened in the most avant-garde manner by the Tradescants. The landscaping of the 1630s at the Earl of Arundel's favourite country retreat at Albury in the Tillingbourne valley has been captured by Wenceslaus Hollar's etchings. These great men's houses and gardens influenced many lesser. Defoe noted that 'The ten miles from

58 *George Lambert's* Wotton Park *(1739), showing John Evelyn's landscaping. His grandson, Sir John Evelyn, carried on his grandfather's tradition, raising beech and fir seedlings 'being the best in my observation, as flourishing as any I have seen in this country'.*

59 *Wenceslaus Hollar's etching of Albury (c.1640) renders a nostalgic 'gentleman's' idea of Surrey country-side. It is remarkable as the very first effective representation of Surrey landscape and is evidence of landscaping at Albury before John Evelyn's (see frontispiece).*

Guildford to Leatherhead make one continual line of gentlemen's houses ... and their parks and gardens almost touching one another.'

Many of the evergreen plants required by the parterres and flowering 'wildernesses' of these formal gardens were cultivated and distributed from specialist nurseries in Thames-side Surrey and Middlesex. They flourished there as Sir William Temple noted partly because of the 'heat-island' created by the extra warmth of the city fires. Certainly the purer air to the west of London would have been very beneficial to horticulture. The Tradescant nurseries at Lambeth were the most famous, being full of exotic plants from Africa, Asia and the Americas which they themselves brought back from their voyages of plant discovery.

Evelyn's Garden Design and Estate Management

The landscaping by the brothers Evelyn which made Wotton the most famous garden in England in the mid-17th century is recorded by John Evelyn in the *Diary* and in his own etchings. John Evelyn's first garden alterations were made when he was only 23 years old in 1643, after the death of his father, and on his return from his first continental tour. 'I built, by my brother's permission, a study, made a fish-pond, an island, and some other solitudes and retirements at Wotton', he wrote. The main reshaping at Wotton appears to have been in 1652-3 when the Civil War was over and John Evelyn had made a Grand Tour embracing Italy and Paris. With his brother's willing help, John then became engrossed in fur-nishing Wotton with 'all the amenities of a villa and garden after the Italian manner ...'. Wotton was then re-shaped on the lines which have basically survived to this day. He dug into the side of the sand hill overshadowing the house on the south for the site of parterres. The spoil filled the moat. The steep hill was terraced, a fountain was supplied by an aqueduct from the river Tillingbourne, and a tree-covered mount was fashioned above a splendid temple. An avenue of Spanish chestnut trees, then 'all the mode for the avenues to their country places in France', extended southwards towards Leith Hill and several grottoes were provided. A *Hortus hyemalis*, or winter garden, prepared with plants that John Evelyn had brought back from Padua, was also added.

Another famous garden designed on Italian lines by John Evelyn was at Albury Park. Under 1667, John Evelyn entered in his *Diary*: 'I accompanied Mr. Howard to his villa at Albury, where I designed for him the plot of his canal and garden, with a crypt through the hill'. He returned three years later to find the canal under construction and the vineyard planted as he had designed it and the then unique crypt (called by Evelyn a 'Pausilippe' from the name of the subterranean passage from the famous Grotto di Posilippo near Naples) dug through the hill. All this was to thrill William Cobbett more than 150 years later, especially the terrace, a quarter of a mile long, backed by its yew hedge. This remains the finest survival of Surrey's formal gardens but even so its present aspect gives little idea of Evelyn's idea of Eden because of the devastation of many of the original features of his garden.

In *Memoires for my grandson*, begun in 1704 and written for the edification of his young heir when Evelyn was 84 years old, he advised on the management of the Wotton estate. This is a most vivid account of the life and attitudes of a Surrey country gentleman at the end of the 17th century and gives us a fascinating glimpse of everyday life at Wotton after three generations of family endeavour, as well as being a window into Evelyn's mind. Evelyn is revealed as a very tight-fisted economist who enthusiastically concerned himself in the day-to-day routine of his home, farm, gardens, orchards and woodlands, and who farmed and planted for a vision of England rather than for immediate profit. He shrewdly recommended the tree-planting of timber trees (oak, ash or elm) as 'the only best and proper Husbandry the Estate is capable of ...'. To prevent further reckless destruction of the old forests he ordered his grandson to stoke his stoves with peat dug on the estate, or with sea coal. Evelyn warns his grandson that he should:

> Not let any of your servants under pretence of killing crows and kites to have a Gunn without your special leave, for they will shoote Connys, pheasants, partriges, Hares and other game and sell them unless you or your stuard do not look them ...

and urges that his grandson's wife should

> have the same inspection of her maid servants ... and all its Apartments, Beding, Hangings, Plate, pewter, linnen, Kitchin furniture, laundry, larders, dairy, cellers, even to the Garrets, to mind and keep all tight and to prevent all want and Imbezilment whatsoever by Chare Women and pretended helpers ...

10

Remodelling the Landscape (1740-1840)

The face of Surrey bears the distinguishing marks of generations of landowners striving to achieve ideal forms of landscape by successive designs each overlapping in time and evolving according to changes in taste and in economic and social conditions. The best known are the grass landscaped parks remodelled in the informal naturalist manner of William Kent, 'Capability' Brown and Humphry Repton whose ambition it was to reproduce in the Surrey countryside the romantic kind of scenery around Rome and Tivoli expressed on the canvases of Claude Lorrain and Nicolas Poussin. Yet the laying out of landscape parks by plutocrats was only one of a number of artistic responses to the exceptionally varied landscape of Surrey. An alternative style of created landscape was the ornamental farm (*ferme ornée*) or the ornamental cottage (*cottage ornée*) which, contrived on the principle of beauty-in-use, was both cheaper and more practical than a park. This was eminently suitable for the retired businessman from London, who during the Regency was 'running up' picturesque cottages and *fermes ornées* along the turnpikes between London and the coast. Meanwhile many country landowners had begun to advance the visual arts not only by laying out landscaped parks but by creating wider landscapes by radiating tree planting over the estate at large, or at least over agricultural land visible from the mansion. By opening out prospects in thick woods, or by planting out unsightly views, by heightening the effects of physical features with trees of contrasting shape and by the free planting of native and exotic trees, the more inspired creators on this case closely intertwined the various components of their estate—the country house, garden, park, home farm, woods, tenants' land and village—into a single, all-embracing composition which, pictorially as well as economically, was conceived as indivisible. The effect of these various, contrasting but interconnecting kinds of landscaping activity is the key to the present aspect of Surrey.

Amongst the earliest of the remodelled Surrey landscapes was that of Sir John Evelyn who inherited Wotton from the diarist at the age of twenty-four. A chronology of his gardening can be reconstructed from the weekly letters written, on his instructions, by his bailiff to him in London and from his own journal there is evidence of his changing Augustan sensibility. His initial task completed by 1715 was that of restoring the pre-existing formal garden of his grandfather and his great-uncle George. He then began to

60 *John Evelyn. As diarist, founding member of the Royal Society, connoisseur and landscape gardener, the Surrey which he plunged into the mainstream of European taste was 'the country of my Birth and my Delight'.*

replant the depleted Evelyn woodlands on an heroic scale, transforming Wotton rather like Lord Bathurst at Cirencester Park or Lord Bessborough at Stansted, West Sussex into an extensive forest with rides and glades cut out of it in the manner of Stephen Switzer's 'rural extensive and Forest gardening' (*Ichnographia Rustica*, 1718, 1742). Representative extracts from the bailiff's letters and his journals illustrate this progress:

1709	Robert Lane (his gardener) transplanted 'above 500 trees of several sorts into the hedgerows and more intended'
1710	Walks near the House re-laid with elm
1712	Re-planted Pasture Wood (several hundred acres)
1714	Re-planted Heathy Land Wood (250 acres)
1719	Paid Henry Arge (a tenant) £1 1s. for saving trees in a hedgerow at Hoopwick Farm he was not obliged to
1722	Planted 300 young saplings on Garrot Hill (on high ground near Leith Hill) and 'about 3,000 more are needed'
1724	Began planting at Noones (an arboretum at Friday Street mill-pond)
1729	Visited West End Farm below Leith Hill (a tenant farm) and saw in a coppice not above two acres at least 1,000 tellers.
1730	The 'account of timber' above the hill (i.e. on the sandy flanks of Leith Hill) showed towards the end of his afforestation: oaks, 6,153; beech, 2,907; ash, 589; elm, 114; oak tellers, 30,000. Below the hill the figures were 4,927, 841, 849 and 320 respectively and tellers numbered more than 20,000.
1736	Fir plantations on Leith Hill now extend over 19 acres.

Evelyn's nurseries on his estate became so celebrated that he supplied many thousands of trees to neighbouring estates when interest in pictorial landscape gardening was beginning to develop and Wotton should thus be seen as one of the mainsprings of a landscaping movement which eventually modified much of Surrey and the entire character of rural England. As early as 1715 Evelyn had supplied 3,400 beech from his own raising to John Parker of Neden. By 1723 he was growing both beech and fir from seed and had supplied large quantities to Sir Edward Nicholas of East Horsley. King George II's estates were also in receipt of trees from Wotton, as was Henry Pelham's Esher Place, and Thomas Moore's Polesden Lacey. The longest connection between Wotton and another 'improving estate' was with the Duke of Newcastle's Claremont. Between 1731, when an annual despatch of tree plants to the Duke was already an established custom, and 1746 there is scarcely a year when Claremont was not supplied with trees by Evelyn. In 1731, for example, the Duke of Newcastle's gardener was supplied with 1,000 chestnuts and on other occasions with two hundred or more beech and oak.

The 'arcadian' Thames from Hampton to Kew became the cradle of English landscape gardening. When William Gilpin, the celebrated writer on the 'Picturesque' and his brother, the artist Sawrey Gilpin, rowed down the Thames between Windsor and London in 1746, the Thameside west of London was even then no longer truly rural. The simplicity of the former

61 *The Hon. Charles Hamilton, the designer of Painshill Park. A portrait by William Hoare of Bath, 1774.*

natural meadows had gone and every foot of land on both the Surrey and Middlesex banks of the river Thames displayed 'an air of high improvement, expense and splendour'. Henrietta Pye's journey in 1760 along the great thoroughfare of the Thames in the vicinity of Richmond and Twickenham led to the discovery of a string of luxury villas which made the whole river a continuous garden or a continuous town, according to whether you appreciated the more the landscaping, as did Henrietta Pye, or the social life, which was Walpole's preference.

Here the greatest amount of land under royal control had been reserved for hunting. In 1637 Charles I extended Richmond Park to 2,500 acres, now not only a remarkable green 'lung' but a haven for wildlife. This stretch of the river Thames is also famous for the outstanding quality of the architecture of the royal palace, the Tudor and Wren Palace at Hampton Court; the great castellated Syon House for Protector Somerset; 17th-century Ham House, home of Charles II's most important minister; the gem of a Palladian villa at Marble Hill for George II's mistress; Horace Walpole's unique fantasy of Strawberry Hill; and Princess Augusta's pagoda at Kew. Understandably this stretch of the river has attracted poets, painters, actors and composers since at least the 16th century. Some of the most powerful figures in the landscape movement have associations here, notably James Thomson, author of *The Seasons*, Alexander Pope, Horace Walpole, and J.M.W. Turner. Turner's idealised view of Thomson's 'matchless Vale of Thames' from Richmond Hill is the supreme picturesque eulogy of this collective waterside landscape. Earlier Richard Wilson had sought out Claudian riverside scenes.

One of the first and most celebrated of Surrey's new informal garden landscapes was laid out between 1738 and 1773 over some 200 acres by the Hon. Charles Hamilton of Painshill Park, Cobham. He created out of an unpromising site of barren heathland a beautiful varied landscape rivalling Stourhead and Stowe, which many 18th-century visitors compared with Elysium and Eden. Hamilton composed the pleasure gardens as a series of pictures which altered continually by surprises and illusions around a lake which was made to seem bigger than it actually was by its shaping and arrangement of islands so that the water could not be seen all at once. Set scenes were centred on temples and follies and paths were skilfully contrived to give the visitor different perspectives and angles from which to view the lake. Tree plantings played their part in concealing a view until it appeared to its best advantage. Painshill was also very much a garden of 'mood' which changed from one part of the garden to another. Hamilton was a keen and adventurous planter, making use of new species discovered in North America. Many of these were planted in open parkland in a free and natural style with 'clumps' in a manner to be adopted later by 'Capability' Brown. The individual buildings included the temple of Bacchus with a ceiling and pedestals by Robert Adam, a gothic temple acting as a focal point commanding magnificent views of the grounds, a 'ruined' Gothic abbey, a Roman mausoleum, a Turkish tent in blue and white and a watch tower from which extensive views to Windsor Castle and to St Paul's could be seen. Other striking features were the Chinese bridge and grotto. Hamilton constructed water wheels to raise water from the river Mole into the lake. The present wheel, 36 ft. in diameter, is dated to 1830 and is one of the first examples of cast iron in gardens.

Until the restoration of Painshill by the Painshill Park Trust from 1981 the garden was virtually derelict. The conservation of the magic pictur-esque scenes at Painshill which so captivated William Gilpin and Horace Walpole is one of the most exciting successes of post-war restoration by a local authority, Elmbridge District Council, working in conjunction with other bodies and has involved extensive archival and documentary research, accurate surveys of the past garden and the meticulous re-building of all its many features.

Amongst the earliest of the Surrey works of art were the influential landscapes of Claremont and Esher owned by the Whig leader, the Duke of Newcastle, and his brother, Henry Pelham, respectively. Of the latter place, only Wayneflete's 15th-century tower survives. Claremont bears the marks of four famous designers: Vanbrugh, who built the original house and laid out formal gardens within massive bailey-like walled defences and a fort-like belvedere tower; Bridgeman, who designed the amphitheatre and converted the walled parterre into a ha-ha (1715-26), but leaving traces of Vanbrugh's work which are traceable to this day; Kent (1738), who de-signed the rectangular lake, cascade, and arranged trees in informal groups; and 'Capability' Brown, who extended the part and added more water features. The landscaped gardens are owned by the National Trust who have undertaken much restoration, tree surgery and re-planting, so reveal-ing to its full effect this important 18th-century landscape garden.

A cheaper and more practical precept of design in landscape which contributed to the re-facing of Surrey was the *ferme ornée* (ornamental or

62 *Painshill landscape. This early 19th-century engraving by G.F. Prosser reveals Hamilton's skilfully-designed landscape garden evoking a series of moods and sensations by means of sudden changes of scenery, interspersed with architectural features. The whole garden was presented as a series of living pictures to be viewed as if one was walking around an art gallery, pausing at each painting (Forge, 1986, 15).*

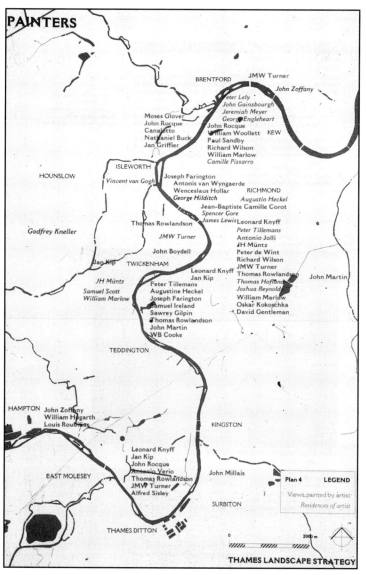

PAINTERS

BRENTFORD   JMW Turner
                                                John Zoffany
                                        Peter Lely
                                      John Gainsbourgh
                                      Jeremiah Meyer
                                      George Engleheart
Moses Glover   John Rocque
John Rocque   William Woollett   KEW
Canaletto   Paul Sandby
Nathaniel Buck   Richard Wilson
Jan Griffier   William Marlow
                         Camille Pissarro
        ISLEWORTH
HOUNSLOW   Joseph Farington
       Vincent van Gogh Antonis van Wyngaerde
                      Wenceslaus Hollar   RICHMOND
                    George Hilditch   Augustin Heckel
                              Jean-Baptiste Camille Corot
                              Spencer Gore
                       James Lewis Leonard Knyff
         Thomas Rowlandson   Peter Tillemans
Godfrey Kneller   Antonio Jolli
            JMW Turner   JH Müntz
                                        Peter de Wint
           John Boydell   Richard Wilson
                                        JMW Turner
Jan Kip   Leonard Knyff Thomas Rowlandson
       TWICKENHAM   Jan Kip   Thomas Hofland
                         Peter Tillemans Joshua Reynolds   John Martin
JH Müntz   Augustine Heckel
Samuel Scott   Joseph Farington William Marlow
William Marlow   Samuel Ireland   Oskar Kokoschka
                         Sawrey Gilpin   David Gentleman
                         Thomas Rowlandson
                         John Martin
                         WB Cooke

        TEDDINGTON

HAMPTON John Zoffany
         William Hogarth
         Louis Roubiliac
                                    KINGSTON

        Leonard Knyff
        Jan Kip
        John Rocque
        Antonio Verio
EAST MOLESEY Thomas Rowlandson John Millais
        JMW Turner
        Alfred Sisley
                          SURBITON

        THAMES DITTON

Plan 4   LEGEND
Views painted by artist
Residences of artist

0   2000 m

THAMES LANDSCAPE STRATEGY

63 *With the Thames as the inspiration, more than 150 writers and poets, designers, architects, painters and musicians created in the 18th century a cradle of English landscape gardening which is acknowledged as one of England's contributions to European art.*

villa farm) which was not so much a business as an essay in the Picturesque. In the *ferme ornée* the farm offices were often joined to the house and the grounds were laid out with a view to utility as well as beauty.

It was Philip Southcote's achievement to change completely the visual relationship of garden and farmland by adopting as his basic principle Addison's *Spectator* pronouncement (1712) that tree planting and other embellishments should be extended into fields and meadows 'so that a man might make a pretty landskip of his own possessions'. Little now survives recognisably of his work at Woburn Farm, near Chertsey, but from Thomas Whateley's description in *Observations on Modern Gardening* we can make a reconstruction. The ornamental farm contained 150 acres, of which 35 were 'adorned to the highest degree', the remainder being a working farm.

In the second half of the 18th century, the rather elaborate ornamentation of Southcote gave way to a simpler and more obviously useful type of ornamented farm. Thomas Ruggles, an able Surrey and Suffolk farmer, devoted much attention to this topic in the 1780s. He advocated a turreted ornamental farmhouse surrounded by woodland opened up by wide rides to give prospects of near farm cottages and well-bred livestock. He advised the repair of old hedges with whitethorn, crab, holly, sweet briar, and honeysuckle, and suggested that single trees planted out of the way of the plough in the 'short lands' of the fields should include Scots pine, larch, silver fir and Weymouth pine. He recommended trees natural to watersides—aspen, white poplar, Carolina pine and Lombardy poplar to improve meadows and brooks. It is this vision of a new Surrey landscape based on the free planting of trees, adopted by so many past Surrey landowners, that has imparted such a widespread glory to the county.

An example of Ruggles' model of a *ferme ornée* was Thorncroft in the Vale of Mickleham. The mansion, built in 1766 on an ornamented estate

64 *The restoration by the National Trust of Charles Bridgeman's turf amphitheatre at Claremont Landscape Garden, formerly hidden by undergrowth and large trees, won an international conservation award.*

of 121 acres, was laid out in regular 14- to 16-acre fields, well planted up with trees and luxurious hedgerows. Its former atmosphere is perhaps well preserved in the exquisite and ingenious map of F.T. Young (1822), itself a minor work of art. This depicts in perspective view the variegated autumn foliage of its hedges, spiked with poplar and conifers, and tree-shrouded farm buildings reflected in the waters of the river Mole.

65 *William Kent, who began landscaping at Claremont in 1729, made Bridgeman's garden much less formal, enlarging and serpenting the pool, and building a classical pavilion on an island. In Horace Walpole's famous phrase, he also 'leaped a fence and saw that all nature was a garden' by designing the ha-ha along the edge of the intensively-modelled garden, to throw it open to the beech plantations on its perimeter.*

11

The Remaking of the Road System and new Forms of Transport (to 1840)

Until the late 18th century Surrey had no effective means of communication with London nor between its neighbouring towns. So appalling were the ways across the Surrey Weald, especially in West Surrey, that for several months of the year farmers had no ready access to markets. John Burton's travel through Surrey and Sussex *c.*1730 was made memorable by his arduous journey over the clays. In the words of another 18th-century observer, wagons dragged along by some means or another through the Weald clay were abandoned the whole winter if they stuck in the autumn mires. John Mechi, a successful businessman and reforming farmer, never forgot his father's struggles early in the 19th century to convey his corn to Guildford market by pack-horse along rough bridle-roads, impassable to wheeled traffic. In wet weather such ways were also utterly unusable by horse. On the drier ridges the going was easier but linking by-roads over the soft rocks of the chalk or Lower Greensand ridge were hollowed out into deeply-rutted narrow tracks along which the saddle-horse was normally the only practicable form of transport. Away from the market towns generally the roads deteriorated and horse riders abandoned them for a course over farmland. Even on the margins of London the badness of the ways near Epsom had emptied the spa of its visitors in autumn and later the roads there were still in poor condition. Malcolm noted in 1805 that 'in following the line of road down Balham Hill we find it in the summer deep in dust and in the winter as deep in mud and so it continues the whole way to Mitcham'.

66 This obelisk at Cranleigh marks the ecstatic relief of a community at their 'rescue' by a new road across some of the most appalling country in winter.

The worst roads of all were in the Weald. Marshall in 1798 declared that, apart from a few public roads, the Weald was roadless. Malcolm observed:

> Who would have believed that it was necessary within thirty miles of London to take a guide, and that with good horses we had much difficulty to ride six miles in four hours and yet that literally was the fact in going from Ockley to Rudgwick.

and in the 1820s Cobbett encountered the deepest clay he had ever experienced in his travels at Ewhurst.

Thus long stretches of Surrey roads before the Age of Improvement were not usable as wagon- or carriage-ways and a regular service of carriers was non-existent. This lack of good roads prevented Surrey from establishing close links with the Metropolis, despite its proximity.

Farmers were placed at a disadvantage in several ways. Wheat, for example, fetched lower prices at Horsham than at Guildford market because Horsham had no water carriage and it was estimated that fat steers walked to Smithfield in the traditional way 'on the hoof' lost three to four per cent in weight during the journey. The economic effects of good turnpikes on Surrey agriculture must not, however, be over-estimated; not until railways were built and the local roads were effectively improved could most farmers really take full advantage of the nearness to London.

By the mid-18th century these deficiencies were acknowledged to be a great obstacle to economic advancement. A necessity began to be felt for better means of communication, especially between London and the coast, for which no good routes existed. Surrey, as has been related, was becoming a favoured place of residence by people who required convenient access to London. Carriage wheels pressed hard upon the heels of the roadmakers, and new mansions sprang up along, or near, ways provided with smooth, hard surfaces. Moreover, Surrey came to lie athwart two of the busiest routes in England: to Portsmouth, an increasingly important naval base and to Brighton and other seaside watering places, which from the social movement of sea bathing for health became fashionable amongst the wealthy. These resorts required for success new roads providing direct access to London. To this end the various turnpike trusts competed with one another to provide the best road services, the easiest gradients, the most direct and best hostelleried routes between main towns and London. This competition had by 1820 created the best road system in Europe.

The successive developments of this new road system tell a particularly fascinating story in Surrey because by the then rising standards of road transport many stretches of its roads were considered too slow or unsafe for stage coaches driven at the ever-faster speeds in vogue. The lie of the land was a basic cause of difficulty. For generations travellers by saddle-horse had instinctively made for higher ground on the ridgeways. This was responsible for steep gradients and circuitous courses around hillsides which were obviated by direct and better graded new routes. Hence the county furnishes many instances of the abandonment of long stretches of former roads. These obsolete ways are one of the most distinctive and charming features of the Surrey landscape.

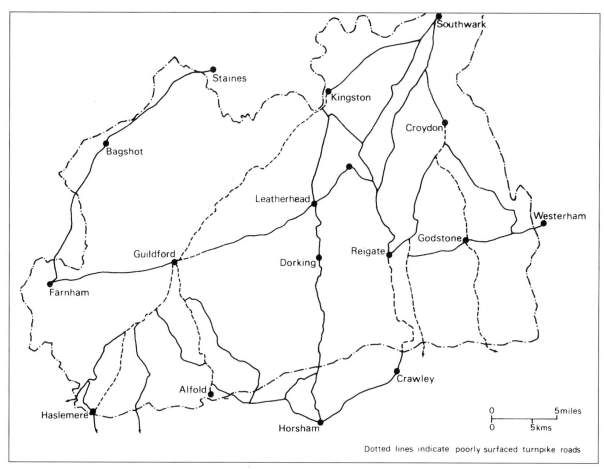

Dotted lines indicate poorly surfaced turnpike roads

67 *Turnpike roads in Surrey. Information as to the condition of the surface is based on James Malcolm, A Compendium of Modern Husbandry, vol.111 (1805), pp.311-23.*

Britannia Depicta (1720), an improved edition of Ogilby's road-book, records only four high roads traversing appreciative stretches of Surrey. Of these two, the Portsmouth and the Old Lewes roads were very ancient lines of communication. The latter ran first to Croydon, then followed the Caterham valley, and thence over the chalk escarpment to Godstone where, unlike the present road, it took the direct line over Tilburstow Hill. This road, in Aubrey's phrase, was 'the great road into Sussex'. Besides Lewes, the ancient ports of Shoreham and Pevensey were served by branches of this road, and in the mid-18th century it became one of the routes to the young seaside resort of Brighton. A third road marked in *Britannia Depicta* was from London to Arundel which ran from Epsom over the Mickleham Downs to Dorking and thence over the sand hills by Coldharbour, to fall steeply from Leith Hill just west of Anstiebury Camp. The fourth route was the cross-road from Godalming on the Portsmouth road to Petworth and Chichester. This climbed steeply out of the Wey Valley and ran over hilly country to Hambledon Common.

This dearth of public roads was replaced within a century by virtually a new system of direct trunk routes between London and the coast and also by a close network of cross-country connections. The first stretch of Surrey road to be improved was the 10 miles between Reigate and Crawley, authorised in 1696 as a saddle-horse road and not improved for carriages until 1755. In 1820 this stretch was again improved by lowering the gradient of Reigate Hill, piercing a sand ridge at Reigate by a tunnel and by a more direct route between Sidlow Bridge and Povey Cross. The deserted older route can be traced curving to the east over Horse Hill and this still remained the only practical way when the river Mole was in flood. These and similar improvements to 'Cockney highways' were stigmatised by William Cobbett in his familiar measured terms.

68 *Bonnetted freight waggon—early 19th century (after J.M.W. Turner).*

Various other coaching roads through Surrey were made to Brighton. The old way, via Godstone, for example, was improved by avoiding the climb over Tilburstow Hill. An alternative route was by Epsom, Dorking and Horsham. The Vale of Mickleham first became an important thorough-fare on this route in 1755 when the road between Epsom and Horsham was turnpiked. In earlier times the 'winter' road to London was so frequently obstructed by the flooding of the river Mole that coachmen and carriers preferred to come over the North Downs by way of Sutton and Betchworth. Another improved coast road was the hilly Dorking-Coldharbour stretch, abandoned for a fine new route over the Holmwood (the present A23 road). The alternative road (regularly used in Evelyn's day) up Wolven's lane and over the chalk escarpment to Leatherhead was abandoned at the same time. The new road authorised in 1764 between Milford and Chiddingfold left completely deserted the stretch between Hambledon Common and North Bridge.

The main alteration to the Portsmouth road was between Thursley and Hindhead in 1826. The old track will be found by Thursley church. Another interesting new coaching road in Surrey was that made from Epsom to Guildford under Acts of 1755-8. The new road ran directly across the fields, leaving the villages along the springline connected by the superseded loops of the old road. The continuation of this road from Guildford to Farnham resulted in the abandonment in 1758 of the steep grass-grown track expressively known as 'The Mount'.

These were some of the smooth Surrey roads along which the stage coaches 'raced' at 12 miles per hour, leaving only 20 minutes on the road for passengers to snatch a hurriedly-eaten but gargantuan meal in the staging inns on the route. Despite the building of railways they carried little local goods traffic until the 1870s. Until this time, for example, the Dorking and Epsom carrier made his regular journeys through Surrey villages to and from the *George* inn in the Borough, the enthrallingly noisy scene commemorated by Dickens.

A number of inns retain enough of their appearance in the coaching era to enable us to recapture the busy scenes when ostlers, working as furiously as present-day teams at motor-racing pit-stops, would replace four tired coach-horses with fresh ones in little more than two minutes. The *Grey-hound* and *Eagle* at Croydon, the *Swan* at Reigate, the *White Horse* at Dorking, made famous by Jane Austen's *Emma* and Dickens' Samuel Weller,

69 *Sussex and Surrey waggoner in the Borough, Southwark.*

and the *George* at Crawley and *Spread Eagle* at Midhurst (Sussex) come readily to mind.

Although main highways were subject to improvement, the local parish roads remained deplorable for much longer. Malcolm listed Surrey parishes with local roads as bad as 'some of the most inaccessible and uninhabited parts of Ireland', including not only most of the Weald parishes, but even those linking well-filled villages on the edge of London, such as Camberwell, Peckham, Wandsworth and in the Kingston district.

Malcolm noted that 'if roads do not happen to lead to a gentleman's house, in the worse order and more impassable are they, and the lower will be the rents of the farms'. His observation that in Surrey generally rents fell within increasing distance to London, those of farms within the innermost ring of up to an half-hour's drive from Stone's End in Kennington being almost double the rentals in an outer zone of up to one hour's distance and six times as much as those in remoter parts, anticipates von Thünen's well-known doctrine of the economic zoning by rings. In districts badly served by roads, agricultural rentals could not be sustained at the general level for the zone. Some of these strips of still working landscape, served only by deeply worn tracks and left aside by the high-roads, did not attract Cockney immigrants until they fell progressively within the purview of villa builders with the advent of railways and further road improvements.

70 *Reigate, archway covering improved road to London.*

In the story of improved communications in Surrey the Wandle valley has a special place, for its important waterside industries induced Croydon businessmen at the beginning of the 19th century to consider a tramway as a better means of conveying passengers and goods to and from London. In Cobbett's day the Wandle valley was one of the most industrialised districts in England, only paralleled by the rapidly developing textile area of Lancashire and West Yorkshire. James Malcolm, who considered the little river as the hardest worked in the world, enumerated in his *Compendium* 39 industrial premises on a nine-mile stretch of the river in 1805, including 16 calico printing and bleaching works, nine flour mills (including exceptionally large premises working several pairs of stones), five snuff mills, four oil-seed crushing mills and a paper mill, saw mill, copper refinery, an iron works and a brewery. For all this industrial development the great market of London was, of course, responsible. Many of the watermills were still standing in the early years of this century. The water cornmills were tending to become ever larger units by the device of building additional water wheels of larger dimensions supplied by re-circulating water between the wheels. Shortly before 1826, for example, Home Pitt Mill at Wandsworth was adapted from a two-wheel mill working eight pairs of 'French' stones to a three-wheel mill working 11 pairs.

In 1802 the Grand Surrey Iron Railway was built from a wharf at the confluence of the Wandle and Thames at Wandsworth. Despite its grand title, this was really a short horse-drawn tramway, but it is noteworthy as the very first publicly-owned conveyance in England. In 1810 it was extended over the Downs to Bletchingley to serve the chalk quarries and Fuller's Earth pits at Merstham and Nutfield. A little older than the tramway

71 Angel Hotel, *Guildford. A fine example of a Georgian inn made prosperous by the new network of turnpikes.*

was a branch of the Grand Surrey Canal cut from New Cross where it joined the main canal. This was designed by Rennie in 1800 and drew water from the Thames by pumping. The canal never prospered and in 1834 the newly-formed London to Croydon Railway bought it up and laid a railway track along its bed from London Bridge. This ultimately became a branch of the London-Brighton railway.

Yet another new transport development was the extension of the Wey Navigation. Built by an Act of Parliament in 1651 it was one of the oldest built waterways in England. By short-cutting bends with lengths of canal and inserting locks, it became possible for barges from the Thames at Weybridge to reach Town Wharf at Guildford. This brought much prosperity to the town: a levy of 1d. on every load (25 cwt.) in 1794 was enough to pave the streets. The Wey Navigation was extended to Godalming in the late 18th century and the Arun Navigation extended to Wisborough Green. In 1816 the Wey and Arun Canal was opened as the connecting link between these canal systems, so providing an inland route between London and Portsmouth, via the Chichester Canal. The canal left the Wey at Stonebridge Wharf, Shalford, and rose by seven locks to Cranleigh, the summit level, and thence passed through a cutting at Alfold before rapidly descending by 16 locks to Loxwood en route to Newbridge, where it joined the Arun Navigation. The person most identified with the canal was George O'Brien Wyndham, the third Earl of Egremont (1751-1837), who during his long and influential life at Petworth espoused the cause of, and committed his large fortune to, agricultural improvement. The canal was never a commercial success, and after 55 years of desultory activity it was closed down. Only a few fragments of masonry or of old timbers now mark the site of the locks. Parts of the canal have been restored for pleasure purposes by the Wey and Arun Trust.

12

Agriculture (1780-1860)

From an agricultural point of view, Surrey was not greatly an 'improving' county. Everyone connected with farming had heard of the Earl of Leicester's agricultural revolution in west Norfolk, the famous four-course arable system of Kent, or the legendary breeding of Southdown sheep on the Sussex Downs, but apart from excellent Dorking fowls, the neat hop-gardens around Farnham and the productive market gardens on London's borders, farming in Surrey had little to excite and much to be deplored.

William Stephenson in his *General View of the Agriculture of the County of Surrey* (1815) estimated that about one-sixth of the county was not then farmed at all, being commons, wastes, landscape parks etc., much of it comparatively worthless from an agricultural point of view. On pleasure farms agriculture was secondary to amenity and Surrey, with soils tending to be mediocre to poor, had no extensive tracts reclaimable or great breadths of arable where a uniform system was carried on. Surrey was thus by no means remarkable as an agricultural county.

The Surrey Weald had little farming that was attractive. Stephenson reported 'scarcely a vestige of improvement' in any part of the Weald in 1813 and that 'everything in it wears the look of inadequate capital and labour misapplied'. William Marshall had been equally scathing a little earlier. Excepting the public road between Petworth and Godalming and Horsham and Dorking he wrote that the central Weald was without roads, 'lanes, yes, but worn into gullies and trodden into sloughs in winter, barely passable. With good roads and a suitable farming practice the Weald lands could be raised to twice their value'. Here extraordinary human exertion was expended on cold, obdurate, begrudging soils with little, undrained fields 'housed-in' with trees. Moreover, there were few passable roads to market, only clay lanes through which horse and man could hardly travel for many weeks of the year. Inevitably, a tenant farmer had to go on summer fallowing for wheat, had to be content with few or no green crops and could keep but little livestock. Thus although the Surrey Weald abounded in beautiful scenery, much owing to its thickly wooded appearance, to the farmer it told a story of smothered crops, half-filled barns, severe under-employment and at best part-time farming.

Fifty years after Stephenson's Report, Surrey farming showed considerable improvement, though this remained unspectacular. 'Making two blades of grass grow where but one grew before' meant that many shaws—belts of timber around fields—had to be cut down, grubbed and cultivated and many small fields enlarged by throwing down hedges and fences.

> There are many farms of 80 to 100 acres with not a field on them containing more than five acres, these little enclosures of the most irregular shapes must be ploughed at great and needless expense; but a still greater evil is that their productiveness is destroyed by over much shade and moisture, as the wide, straggling shaws never allow the sun to shine on them except for a few hours in the middle of the day ...
>
> (Siday Hawes of Horsham [1853]).

Shaws also encouraged the growth of weeds and couch on the head-lands, and harboured vermin such as rabbits and slugs. Evershed of Albury described the change by 1853 as 'immense' and that 'all but the tourist may be delighted by the sight of hedges and timber falling in all directions', though in 1858 Siday Hawes of Horsham stated that the process of hedge-row and shaw removal had not gone far enough and to this day the Surrey Weald retains something of its distinctive character of a patchwork of small wood-bounded fields.

Local roads by this time had been greatly improved but under-draining the fields, the cheapest and most durable improvement on heavy land, was

72 *Scharf's sketch of flare limekilns with bottle-shaped chimneys at the foot of the North Downs near Dorking (1823). During the course of the 17th century liming the cold clays of Surrey Weald had displaced marling to some extent. This resulted in the working of huge chalk quarries, especially between Dorking and Reigate.*

near Dorking   g. Scharf del. 1823

going on but slowly in the mid-19th century. The recent invention of making draining pipes by machinery had cheapened the expense and accelerated the process of making the claylands grow all that they were capable of. Farmers continued to ridge-up their arable giving the appearance of a gigantic corrugated draining board and this traditional method of draining for crops is readily traceable on tumbled-down grassland which has been infrequently ploughed since the farming depression from the 1880s. On the sandlands considerable enclosure and cultivation had lessened their great extent noted by Stephenson. This was particularly so on the Bagshot Sands centred on Bagshot. Here the process of improvement consisted in paring, burning the heath and trenching, by spade or pick, to the depth of 20 inches to break through the 'iron crust' which is invariably found under sand and which, being impervious to water, caused heaths to be frequently wet and boggy.

73 *Castle Mill, Dorking, on the river Mole in the shadow of Box Hill is one of numerous mills re-built or enlarged to cope with rising agricultural production.*

Marshall, in 1791, had claimed that there were so few roads over the heaths of south-west Surrey that they were 'as difficult of access as the mountains of Merionethshire or Perthshire' and notwithstanding their location with respect to the metropolis they were in their present state 'the most unprofitable to the country of any district of equal extent, with Ireland and the Scottish Highlands excepted'. By the 1850s it was accepted that the heaths of Frensham, Witley and Thursley and those of Frimley, Woking and Bagshot consisted of sterile and unimprovable sand and so must ever remain irreclaimable.

With the coming of the railway, chalk was brought from Basingstoke to stations along the line to Waterloo and passenger trains collected vegetables and milk for the Waterloo terminus. This facility had a marked effect on dairying and on the cultivation of carrots and peas along land served by the railway and, had the milk retailing been better organised, London could have been provided with more good milk without farmers being engaged in an often troublesome and profitless affair with those who hawked it about the streets. Another boon was the manure brought from London by railways to Surrey farms, including guano, superphosphate, malt-dust, bonedust, ashes, salt, soot and dung, which was applied on land for green crops.

Some parts of Surrey were noticeably better farmed than the average. The Guildford district, largely on chalky soils, and the Mole valley at Cobham and Stoke D'Abernon, enriched by calcium washed down by the river Mole, were singled out. The agricultural writer William Marshall was also impressed at the end of the 18th century by the Farnham hop-farmers. Hop-growing had been celebrated here for centuries and had spread to Wrecclesham, Bentley and on to Alton in Hampshire. The fertility was largely from the chalkiness of the soil. The trained thorn or lime trees planted in close rows to shelter the hops made the Vale of Farnham one of the most beautiful in Surrey. Marshall pointed out that the method of cultivating hops was different at Farnham from that at Cranbrook or Maidstone in Kent, a still more important centre. At Farnham cultivation was done by manual labour, not by horse-drawn implements and the hops were grown on fewer poles than in Kent and harvested at an earlier stage of ripeness. Great care was taken with the produce and so Farnham hops fetched a higher price than Kentish. The wagons taking hops to Weyhill Fair, some thirty miles west, returned with cheeses and other dairy produce. Hop-pickers celebrated the end of the season by dancing in the streets of Farnham to the music of fiddlers and, bedecked in ribbons and coloured handkerchiefs, returning to their home villages in wagons carrying thirty to forty persons, 'altogether a sort of glee and merriment' rarely met with.

After passing through busy Croydon, the coach traversed a rich hay and dairying belt on wet, cold clays, but ameliorated with copious London dung. At the fifth milestone from London Bridge, the farms disappeared and nurserymen, gardeners and cow-keepers were interspersed between brick-makers and the scattered residences of London business men as far as Brixton Causeway. The most delightful nursery gardens were those growing plants for the perfumer and chemist. Mitcham and Sutton were famous for lavender, peppermint, camomile, liquorice, poppy and musk-roses. Oils were distilled on the nurseries which were dependent on huge quantities of London dung.

On Surrey estate maps of about 1740 to 1850 there is invariably marked a centrally-placed lime kiln on the wayside. Lime was applied each time acidic land lay fallow, about once in five or six years on the Weald Clay and a little less frequently on the also rather sour Lower Greensand. Until the widespread distribution of lime from the quarry kilns became practicable with the introduction of railways and improved by-ways, almost every farmer on acid soils carted lime to his own kiln. This was built of stone, 18 to 20 feet high, and shaped like a round tower. Earth was heaped around one side to provide a ramp so that the kiln could be fed from the top. The limeburner raked with a long pole the furze or wood fire every 20 minutes or so and rested little during the three-day operation, regularly sending up flames into the darkness. With the introduction of railways agricultural lime was brought from quarries on the escarpment of the North Downs. The quarries in the scarred hillsides at Betchworth and Buckland, visible for miles across the Weald, still characterise these relict industries.

Despite some general progress since Stephenson's *Report* of 1813 observers in the 1850s were still very critical of the backward state of Surrey agriculture. James Caird in his *English Agriculture in 1850-1* took as an illustration the 'undrained marshes, ill-kept roads, untrimmed hedges, rickety farm-buildings, shabby-looking cows of various breeds and dirty cottages' encountered on a walk in the Tillingbourne valley from Gomshall railway station. He attributed most of this neglect to the pernicious custom of letting farms on yearly leases, a practice favoured by tenants who fraudulently 'worked out' a farm and received from an incoming tenant payment for 'imaginary improvements and alleged operations'. This bad system was the staple of numerous Surrey land agents and valuers whose shiny brass plates were a feature of every little town in the county. An exceptional improvement was the farming at Albury of the banker Henry Drummond. He enlarged his park, set out the present estate village, built two churches, a fine Romanesque one for the new village and another in the park for the Apostolic Catholics (Irvingites), leaving the old church a ruin.

13

William Cobbett's Surrey (1780-1840)

Few have looked as long and closely at the landscape of southern England and evoked its spirit so vividly in prose as William Cobbett, who was born in 1762 at Farnham and who died, after repeated travel and adventure, in 1835 at Normandy Farm in Ash, only a few miles from his birthplace. Throughout a lifetime of pugnacious political writing he clung with fanatical devotion to the countryside and way of life of old Surrey which to him were the embodiment of all the traditions and virtues which he cherished as most truly English. From his pen, and especially the hurriedly-written, spontaneous reports he published in *Rural Rides*, we can still capture an extraordinarily fresh and intimate sense of the Surrey scene in the 1820s, all the more because in his quest for first-hand knowledge Cobbett avoided turnpikes and happily took to the byways.

Amongst Cobbett's most vivid picturesque figures in *Rural Rides* are the 'clay and coppice' people inhabiting the Surrey Weald. In this poor and slow-changing countryside the self-supporting peasant was still living close to the soil with his bakehouse, brewhouse, pigsty and rabbit warren. The cheerful, hard-working and comparatively well-off Wealden peasant symbolised his idea of the perfect English countryman. Strong as the soil he worked upon, he still formed part of a recognisable community, all but inaccessible to strangers, still holding his own in the self-sufficiency which was for generations in the Weald a condition of survival. His very dress proclaimed his battle with the soil.

> As 'God has made the back to the burthen', so the clay and coppice people make the dress to the stubs and bushes. Under the sole of the shoe is *iron*; from the sole six inches upwards is a high-low; then comes a pair of leather breeches; then comes a stout doublet: over this comes a smock-frock; and the wearer sets brush and stubs and thorns and mire at defiance.

As one in whom the love of home and family was singularly intense, Cobbett inevitably took pride in the old Surrey farmhouses whose doors, hearths, windows and furnishings of oak tables, oak bedsteads, oak chests of drawers and oak clothes-chests, and the very scent of the air upon them, were to him expressive of all the qualities of an admired inherited past. In their presence Cobbett felt some intangible essence lingering of an earlier, homelier Surrey, and they so vividly recalled to him an association with generations of Surrey folk that we can almost hear the farm labourers

clumping in with their hob-nail boots
and dining cheerily at the side-tables
just as they had done at Thorncroft
centuries earlier (see p.48). In the old
unaltered farmhouses Cobbett had
recovered a trace of the Surrey of
his childhood and nostalgia swept
over him. Hence his inflexible cen-
sure for 'Jews and Jobbers', the most
sinister figures in his Chamber of
Horrors, who were buying up Surrey
farmhouses and building and furnishing in the new-fangled style of the
age. Coming into Surrey in the wake
of this Cockney invasion of the Surrey countryside were *parlours*, 'aye,
and with a *carpet* and *bell-push* too',
mahogany chairs, sofas, fine glass,
wine decanters, dinner and breakfast
sets, dessert knives. Such changes
were to continue long after Cobbett's
death and in time were to envelop all
Surrey. They were to lead to the revivalist houses of the Arts and Crafts
Movement (see Chapter 15).

Cobbett made another encounter
with 'Jobbers' at Croydon, in 'two
entire miles of stock-jobbers' houses',
and again at Reigate where the
Brighton turnpike was being
smoothed and levelled so that they
could 'skip backward and forward
on the coaches and actually carry on
stock-jobbing on "Change Alley"', though they reside in Brighton'.

74 *William Cobbett, most pugnacious of mortals and an inspiring prophet without being given any real credit for it. His vitality was inexhaustible.*

As early as 1825, Cobbett drew a distinction between the unselfcon-
scious face of the traditional Surrey farming landscape and the new gentry's 'artificial' landscape spreading out of London in the wake of the
turnpikes. Sarcastically he cast his exact, quick glance over the 'improvements' which frustrated his express aim to see the county's agriculture and
its working farmers and labourers. The experience of a day's journey in
Surrey led him to conclude that the traditional habits and sights of rural
England survived only along rutted hollow-ways unusable to carriages such
as were around Thursley and Hascombe. Beside the great high roads from
London the new gentry, who were his aversion, were 'expelling' yeomanry
and sensuously rearranging landscape, activities associated in Cobbett's
mind with the topsy-turvydom and trumpery created by the repulsive
eruption of the Great Wen.

Cobbett's distinction between two contending forces in the Surrey landscape, the one sustaining a working landscape of traditional (often mean) farm buildings rented by round-frocked farmers, the other new designs worked upon for pleasure like a piece of stage scenery, is amply borne out by other writers, though not all, of course, would have agreed with Cobbett as to which was the baser and which the better.

One of the earliest Surrey districts to be remade was the Vale of Mickleham, pierced by the river Mole in its passage through the North Downs. Its delightful wooded landscape blends so harmoniously with the contours, and so forgotten is the care lavished upon its making, that such scenery is often wrongly regarded as 'natural' to Surrey. This is the reverse of the truth. Surrey scenery is almost entirely man-made and the most beautiful landscapes are those with a history of landowners who have cared for them. In fact, the Vale in the mid-18th century was then a bare landscape of low-rented rabbit warren and sheepwalk which was remodelled into hanging woods, woodland walks, plantations, parks and ornamental farms after the Vale became readily accessible to London with the opening of the Epsom to Horsham turnpike in 1755. Much of the achievement is due to George Lock who bought the Norbury estate in 1774 and rebuilt Norbury Park immediately afterwards. Lock's landscape room at Norbury Park (c.1775) is one of the finest examples in England of 18th-century rooms painted with continuous landscapes to create the illusion that one is not inside the room but outside, surrounded by the picturesque scenery depicted. The sides of the room open to four views. The windows on the south framed the picturesque scenery then being remade in the Vale of Mickleham. The other walls of the room are generalised paintings of the Lake District by George Barrett (1728-1784). This painted room represents the high watermark in the cult of the Picturesque associated with William Gilpin, who was greatly admired by Lock and whose Western Tour began at Norbury Park.

Soon after the building of Norbury the surrounding hills were crowded with decorative mansions overlooking parks, neat bow-fronted *cottages ornées* and thickly-wooded clumps of yew and box. All these landscape 'effects' spelt death to the old rural customs, especially the exercise of common rights. An example of the changes involved is an agreement made in 1789 between the lord of the manor of Headley and his 17 copy-holders whereby the lord gave up his right to the tenant's best beast on the death of a copy-holder in return for surrender of the traditional right to cut bushes, furze and underwood on the Nower.

So accessible to London was Dorking and the Vale of Mickleham with the building of the London to Worthing road in 1755 that the water-colourist George Scharf used the district below Box Hill to train his son (later the first Director of the Portrait Gallery) in landscape painting (Fig. ??). When mid-19th-century landscape artists became alienated from London and developed to a fanatical degree a passion for 'the country', a few rural districts near London were brought into a general artistic consciousness for the first time. The leading one was the Vale of Mickleham. Before

IX *Witley railway station, as depicted by* Punch, *enabled the creation of an artistic and literary colony which included J.C. Hook, RA, the watercolourist Birket Foster and novelist George Eliot.*

X *Benjamin Williams Leader (1831-1923) moved to Burrows Cross near Shere, built by Richard Norman Shaw for the artist Frank Holl. Leader's popular appeal was enormous and his works must have lured many wealthy migrants to the Surrey heaths.*

XI *Ethelbert White conceived at Shere a fiction of Surrey in his poster of 1925 which was of the kind that yearly imposed its identity on the real Surrey for leisure-seeking townspeople.*

XII *With its population explosion through migrations outwards from London, Croydon has become a city in all but name. The 'Dallas'-style tower-blocks reflect Croydon's stupendous commercial growth in the 1960s and '70s. Despite Croydon's post-war transformation, several old buildings survive, including the archbishop's palace, Whitgift's Hospital and former coaching inns.*

railways widened artists' options, this district became recognised as a suitable trainee-artist's workshop on account of the richly varied and supremely
beautiful wooded course of the river Mole under the slopes of Box Hill,
combined with its accessibility to the capital. This 'improved' landscape
contrasted greatly with the neighbouring North Downs above Reigate and
Godstone. The sparseness of the population impressed the traveller and so
also did the small, neglected churches. The parish of Woldingham contained only two or three farmhouses and a few cottages, and even as late
as 1811, when the Wen was beginning its encroachment, the total number
of its inhabitants was only fifty-eight. Its church consisted of one room
about 30 ft. long and 21 ft. wide, without tower, spire, or bell. Even in
Evelyn's day, it had been dilapidated, desolately standing upon its hill; its
restoration was not undertaken until 1890 when Woldingham was inhabited by villa builders. The appearance of Farleigh was still almost unchanged from its 14th-century aspect as a hamlet on the estate of Merton
College. Its little church had not been structurally altered since 1250. The
Rev. J. Kilner, the rector in 1767, observed that it was a parish of roughly
1,000 acres, but containing only 20 families and a total population of 94,
of which 18 resided at the manor house of Farleigh Court and nine at the
Rectory. He also explained that only half of the arable of 700 acres was
annually under corn: the remainder had to be sown to grass. Yet another
of the thinly-populated parishes on the North Downs was Walton-on-the-
Hill. Its church was declared to be in such a dangerous and dilapidated
condition in 1818 that the Bishop of Winchester granted a faculty to re-
build the church except the chancel and part of the tower. The old church
of Titsey was also pulled down in 1775 and one built in its place was
superseded yet again in 1861 by the present church. The west wall of
Warlingham church, rebuilt in the 17th century, was partially pulled down
in the restoration of 1893-4. These details of church building convey an
impression of the poverty of scantily-populated parishes until the invasion
of London business people from the late 19th century, immortalised by
John Betjeman's *Love in a Valley*.

75 *Improved   sheep,
18th century.*

It was in the Tillingbourne valley that Cobbett made his celebrated
diatribe against 'two of the most damnable inventions that ever sprang
from the minds of man under the influence of the devil', namely the making of gunpowder and of banknotes. The Lower Works of the gunpowder
mill at Chilworth had been converted to paper manufacture at the beginning of the 18th century. Paper-making continued on this site until 1870 at
two mills known as Chilworth Great and Chilworth Little. At Albury Park
Charles Ball took over the former corn mill and rebuilt it as a paper mill
but in the early 1800s Ball's mill was closed when owners of the manor
started to re-settle villagers of the original Albury settlement at Weston
Street, and Ball erected for his sons two new paper mills at Postford, where
paper-making continued until 1875. The other paper mills in Surrey also
began to close at the end of the 19th century, except Catteshall which
closed in 1928.

14

The Land of Heart's Desire (1840-1918)

76 *The willow, Rev. James Dallaway's garden, Leatherhead, c.1821.*

To the Victorian businessman's mind, Surrey was paradisal, the land of his dreams, a great beckoning landscape of verdant charm to which he irresistibly surrendered. Over the length and breadth of Surrey horse-drawn carriages daily came out of trim lodge gates bearing members of the business community towards the nearest railway station to the accompaniment of the distant whistle of a London-bound train. Each evening these excellent men of business 'their names good upon 'Change for anything they chose to put their hand to' returned from their counting house under the soot-laden pall of London leaving only a brass plate to tell the Cockney passer-by where their money was made. With very few exceptions the old great families of Surrey became extinct and their estates passed into the hands of bankers, stockbrokers and distillers.

Country houses, in fact, became an established part of the life of the Victorian middle-class and changed the face of Surrey in a single generation. To select a fair and high locality, not too far away from London, and to make there a modish place where his family could enjoy fresh air and such country luxuries as fresh milk and other farm produce, was the overriding ambition of the successful. London was perceived as so pre-eminently a city *within* doors that only country houses as Victorians knew them were seen to fulfil the requirements for health, recreation and repose. The ownership of land also conferred social and political prestige. It furthermore offered a means of gratifying the aim of the rising Victorian middle class to improve on an inheritance and hand it on for future enlargement. Many Victorian landowners took this rôle so seriously that they considered landownership almost a sacred trust involving responsibility to tenants and staff, as well as providing pleasure.

It needed only one family to discover a secluded village and invite friends to spend the weekend to set off a chain reaction resulting in a number of large country houses springing up, turning it into a chic upper-class residential area. In the exquisite scenery of the two adjoining parishes of Abinger and Holmbury St Mary, for example, new mansions were owned by the heads respectively of the Castle Shipping Line, Doulton's Lambeth and Wedgwood potteries, Stephen's inks, Guinness, Brooke Bond Tea and accountants Price Waterhouse, together with the then Lord Chief Justice, High Court judges, ex-colonial administrators, doctors, artists and architects. Ten large country houses were built in the space of twenty years. Joldwynds (the home of the Queen's oculist) had 26 bedrooms. All possessed extensive gardens and landscape parks, planted with the then popular exotic trees such as monkey puzzles, ginkos and Himalayan rhododendrons. Such houses demanded a large amount of domestic labour, and while many households brought down staff at weekends, there were many jobs available for local people, particularly as gardeners. Waterhouse's Feldemore, for example, had a staff of 11 gardeners and nine domestic servants. Cottages were built in villages to house staff not accommodated in the servants' quarters, shop-keepers migrated to set up business and churches, chapels and schools were erected. George Edmund Street, the architect of the Law Courts in the Strand, built his own country house here and designed the magnificent church. Another instance of major change enveloped the home at Newlands Corner of the editor-proprietor of *The Spectator*, St Loe Strachey. His daughter has written:

> No one who knows the two roads over the hill today can have the slightest idea of what a desolate spot Newlands Corner was in the year 1890. There was no post, there was no water; there was no noise of any sort. Occasionally a cart tumbled past the high hedge which bordered the farmhouse garden, but no one at all seemed to drive up Clandon Hill ...

Here the Stracheys spent weekends for forty years, eulogising 'Its keen, almost mountain air, its views, its woodlands, its yews, its groves of ash and oak and thorn ...'. Strachey erected cheap houses from the Ideal Homes Exhibition to combat the shortage in rural Surrey. In 1908 Clough Williams-Ellis, then a young and unknown architect, accepted Strachey's challenge to better the design. Williams-Ellis added a cheap cottage of his own at Newlands Corner and after the War (now married to Annabel Strachey) he added bungalows in pisé (rammed earth) which are now clad in brick to meet the District Council's regulations.

A quite different colony arose on the flanks of Hindhead. Cobbett inveighed against Hindhead in the spirit of 18th-century agriculturists as the 'most villainous spot God ever made' and amuses us in *Rural Rides* by trying to circumvent its wild and desolate moor associated in travellers' minds with a particularly grisly murder. Yet towards the end of the 19th century its bracing air, intense solitude and some of the most magnificent views in the south of England exercised such influence on Darwinian nature-lovers that the landscape was etherealised into something of the idea of heaven. As did Tennyson on nearby Blackdown, pioneer settlers on Hindhead built themselves houses so as to look upon a supernaturally awe-inspiring panorama, notwithstanding that before the advent of the motor-car the situation was by no means convenient.

The first resident was the eminent Victorian scientist, John Tyndall, who initially built a hut in 1882. When he was building a house the following year Bertrand Russell's uncle Rollo followed in his footsteps. Tyndall's recommendation led to the arrival of Professor Huxley at weekends. 'Wicked people', wrote Tyndall, 'have spread the report that a colony of heathens is being established at Hindhead. *Your* presence here, even for a little while, would complete the evidence.'

This growing colony had suffered from aesthetic starvation in towns. Its residents tended to be pantheistic lovers of nature in the Wordsworthian sense, perceived by local people as eccentrics with 'advanced' ideas, being generally agnostic, eugenicist, suffragist, sexually liberated, devoted to the open air and high standards of craftsmanship of the Arts and Crafts movement.

It was not only the large country house which transformed Surrey landscape and society at this time. Late Victorian gentry spoke of a 'pleasure farm' when they wished to denominate an agricultural estate largely turned over to ornament and leisure. The change in name coincided with a change in taste. The 'pleasure farm' symbolises the pronounced swing of taste to the eclectic and the revivalist forms of architecture. Its dwelling was typically a renovated half-timbered or stone-built yeoman's farmstead or small existing manor house. Such property came cheaply on the market in the last quarter of the 19th century as the prices for heavy land of mediocre quality tumbled with the increasing import of corn from overseas. With the growth of trans-Wealden railways between London and the coast, 'pleasure farms' for sporting purposes became characteristic of the Surrey Weald. Such stretches of low country left most people comparatively unresponsive to its quiet beauty and they did not afford the prospects deemed essential for the perfect villa landscape, so that outwardly the traditional Surrey landscape has survived more than elsewhere. John Ruskin published in *Fors Clavigera* an account of the process which transformed a Surrey working countryside into a 'cocktail belt' with all its resultant social upheaval. A Cranleigh resident reported in 1887 that some years previously 'some manufacturers and others who had made large fortunes in "trade" came to settle in that part of Surrey and bought farms, or hired them for much higher rents than normal'. This led to a rise in land rents for the entire district, putting farmers in great difficulty.

77 *Cheap housing, Merrow Down. By realistic design, architect Clough Williams-Ellis kept costs to a minimum.*

The new masters also paid higher wages than the old and 'not knowing what was a fair day's work permitted less and less ...'. The migrants soon had a new house built about the farm, or were engaged in renovating and enlarging the old, and then induced the parish to make up the green lanes into hard roads at great expense and the consequent increase in the parish rates was another nail in the farmer's coffin.

The growing demand for building land pushed up land prices in general and many cottagers lost their traditional way of life when commons were enclosed and sold off by lords of manors in convenient building lots for purchase. In this way whole

78 *Clough Williams-Ellis' family shanty near Shere, built for week-ending in the early 1920s.*

districts were 'gentrified' and manicured leaving few traces of the old rural society. This was dramatic on the southern flanks of Leith Hill, for example, where the rural population was said to be 'least advanced' in the southern counties, being the worst type of heathmen, smugglers, fugitive settlers, squatters and commoners, as at Peaslake, of which persons in Shere village, then within the same parish, spoke only with horror and despair on account of its lawlessness.

In many parts of Surrey the old rural charm was harmed by insensitive building in materials out of keeping with the locality. Examples can be found, however, of the care exercised by landlords, architects and builders in the siting and construction of country houses. The estate of the Brays of Shere, whose association with the district remains unbroken after five hundred years, is one of these.

Before the First World War Reginald Arthur Bray (1869-1950) and his father Sir R.M. Bray used great discrimination in the matter of land development. They did not sell land for building but instead granted 99-year leases of land after their approval of architects' plans for proposed houses. The minimum amount of money to be expended on the house was specified. By this simple device the Brays were able to impose a strict control on the size, type and design of any dwelling erected on their 4,000-acre estate between *c.*1880 and 1914. By inference from the vernacular style of existing buildings (e.g. Rapsley and Coneyhurst farms) it is clear that their definition of suitability included the stipulation that new buildings should harmonise with older structures and reflect the ancient traditions of the countryside. The general use of building stone from the Bray's own quarries and locally-made brick made this control easier and the employment of a local builder, King

79 *The Hallams, Shamley Green, by Richard Norman Shaw.*

of Abinger Hammer, in whom the Brays had trust, also meant that craftsmen using the methods and styles of former times were generally employed.

In Victorian and Edwardian Surrey the continuous stream of wealth and piety pumped by *nouveaux riches* into a formerly thinly peopled and poorly endowed countryside carried the new movement of church building and restoration to an intensity hardly equalled in any other part of England. Cracklow's famous views of Surrey churches in 1823 show that rural Surrey possessed hardly any large parish churches, unlike many parts of Kent and Sussex where wealth from the wool and iron industries had resulted in church rebuilding in the 15th and later centuries. Typically, Surrey churches were dilapidated patchworks of varying periods, owing partly to the badness of local stone, partly to neglect and partly to injudicious repairs which neglect had brought. Often of considerable charm, they were nevertheless deemed to be no credit to an Age of Prosperity and Progress. Even by Cracklow's day some medieval churches had been completely rebuilt, for example, Holy Trinity, Guildford and the parish churches of Chertsey, Egham and Mitcham; Shalford, Long Ditton and Walton parish churches were rebuilt twice. Very few Surrey churches survive unaltered and many were completely rebuilt in mass imitation of the greater medieval churches of 13th-century France or of the Stone Belt of England, as Ruskin had urged. These were paid for by the new country-house owners and their families. The archaeological loss from insensitive so-called 'restorations' was tremendous. The history of Reigate parish church is typical. In Woodyer's 1845 'restoration' a fine 15th-century window in the nave was replaced by a commonplace Decorated one, an anachronism confusing the history of the church. The interior monuments were treated with a similar disregard; and as a consequence of the decay of the local sandstone ashlar, the most exposed walls, a doorway and even a window were coated with stucco. Gilbert Scott junior's thorough restoration of 1873 was necessary to make the church once more worthy of its site. He rebuilt the noble arcades of *c.*1200 stone by stone and refaced the tower in Bath stone.

80 *Philip Webb, a close friend and partner of William Morris, was the architect responsible for Coneyhurst, Joldwynds and several other Surrey country houses.*

G.M. Young has argued that the social revolution wrought by the new arrivals into the Surrey countryside was to the general benefit. 'Wealthy landowners understanding the economics of agriculture, a farmer master of his practice, a village not over-populated, with pure water, decent houses, allotments and a school, made up the most successful experiment in social organisation that England had so far seen'. But this social upheaval did not go unchallenged for some saw it as meretricious and at the price of uprooting the old social order and destroying much of the traditional landscape and ways of life. George Meredith became increasingly concerned in the 1890s at the 'hectoring of lovely country by hideous villas' and a visit by William Morris to the Wealden oak-country at Witley a little earlier had left him surprised at its being 'amazingly free from anything Cockney-based', though the growing villadom of urban interlopers of Hindhead repelled him. Roger Fry, the leading art critic, who built a villa near Guildford, half-apologised to visitors for a countryside spotted with so many 'gentlemanly residences'.

81   *Pierrepoint, Frensham, by Richard Norman Shaw.*

The glutting of Surrey with commonplace landscaped parks was also a source of criticism, a type of development fostered by sharply falling prices of poorer agricultural land and woodland in the farming depression from the 1870s. Whole areas of Surrey came to be used for ornament and game conservation, with a cow or blade of corn hardly to be seen, to the puzzlement of foreign observers such as Kropotkin. 'The contribution of the average English landscape park to the landscape is notable only for its dullness and monotony', complained *The Spectator* in 1897. By this time George Sturt (Bourne) of Farnham was lamenting the readiness 'to sell or break up or cut down or level away anything on any sites' in Surrey. He deplored the enclosure of commons for building and the way 'the educated, the propertied [acted] towards the uneducated and unpropertied without understanding'. He saw the middle classes wanting to civilise the worker, to 'do him good' and wanting '... to make him more like themselves, and yet keep in his place of dependence and humiliation'.

82   *It was at Flint Cottage, Box Hill, at which George Meredith lived in later life, that he wrote, as recently as 1882: 'Nowhere in England is richer foliage, or wider downs and fresher wood'. These were the very substance of his poetry and of many of his novels.*

These criticisms of the new order intensified in the Edwardian era of 'Land of Hope and Glory' country houses which had taken on an extravagant and ostentatious swagger which by their presence disturbed the economic and social balance of whole districts. The custom of letting country houses to wealthy city men who had no real knowledge of or sympathy with the neighbourhood then became common. It was remarked at this time of this practice that 'the formerly real bond between a landlord and his tenants had then ceased to exist except on a very few estates'. This can be illustrated with reference to Rickettswood in Charlwood, rented in the summer months by civil engineer Lord Rendel. Lady Stocks has written in her autobiography:

> Rickettswood was a closed Rendel community. It had almost no rural contacts with the surrounding countryside. No vicar called. It did not visit neighbouring houses, nor was it visited. Nor did it deserve to be. It was self-sufficient.

15

Building and Gardening in 'Surrey Style'
1870-1939

From the 1860s, when the railways brought Surrey into easy reach of London and the histrionic styles of the Gothic Revival as at Horsley Towers, home of the Earls of Lovelace and originally designed by Sir Charles Barry, were falling into disfavour, the Surrey cottage inspired revivalist architects, notwithstanding their often tumbledown appearance and their bedraggled occupants. Professional architects admired the proportion, balance and graceful simplicity of half-timbered and stone-built houses, and the masterly attention given by traditional builders to details such as chamfers, stops, beams and joints were also noted, as also the way in which most such houses seemed to 'grow' organically from their settings. This heritage of domestic building was used by professionals as models for their own designs which Roderick Gradidge describes as 'rather gawky'. Soon after a deeper understanding of Surrey vernacular is marked by Charles Baily's 'Remarks on Timber Houses' (1869) and Ralph Nevill's *Old Cottage and Domestic Architecture in South-West Surrey* (1889). The latter's work is significant because he was the first Surrey architect who studied and interpreted the Surrey vernacular in connection with his alterations and additions to old houses and Gradidge considers that his drawings had considerable influence on a great number of architects.

By the end of the 19th century numerous architects were handling the Surrey vernacular with flair. The pioneers in this movement were Norman Shaw (1831-1912) and two of his pupils, Mervyn McCartney and Ernest Newton. They recreated the style and building techniques of indigenous southern-English architecture, even to the extent of incorporating open halls, great hearths and chimneys, pargetting, braced beams, immense bay windows, deep cornices and bracketted barge boards. The chief inspiration of these architects for the new type of small country home was the Wealden house and particularly those nearest to London. Young architects wishing to make a national reputation drove a trap or cycled down deep woody Wealden byways searching at every lane's turning for vernacular survivals as models for their pattern books. Shaw, as a young man, worked in the office of G.E. Street, an architect who has left a deep mark on Surrey with his numerous churches and whose home, 'Holmdale' (1873), at Holmbury St Mary is delightfully set on a wooded hillside. Shaw's own flair for recreating comfortable and sensibly planned country houses for the *nouveaux riches* is illustrated by 'Pierrepoint', near Frensham (1870), 'Merrist Wood' near Guildford (1877), 'Burrows Cross' near Gomshall (1885) and 'Hallams', Shamley Green (1894-5).

'Merrist Wood' was one of the first moderately-sized houses to combine half-timbering, tile-hanging and locally quarried Bargate stone in his 'Old English Style'. He built several smaller houses along the Portsmouth Road in Guildford for metropolitan commuters. Burrows Cross was designed for the artist Frank Holl and later occupied by artist Benjamin Leader. These works in many ways anticipate the later vernacular work of Lutyens. This vernacular inspiration was powerfully influenced by the Arts and Crafts Movement led by William Morris. Major figures in this were Philip Webb, C.F.A. Voysey and many less well known yet equally successful architects such as Thackeray Turner, the first professional secretary of the Society for the Protection of Ancient Buildings, C. Harrison Townsend, Baillie Scott, Harold Falkner, who transfigured Farnham, and Curtis Green, a fine architect and draughtsman, who published *Old Cottages and Farmhouses in Surrey* (1908). Meanwhile several artists had introduced the Surrey cottage to the wider public, notably Birket Foster who painted at Witley from the early 1860s and is buried in the churchyard, Helen Allingham who followed him to the same district, and Kate Greenaway; Luke Fildas, Stacy Marks, Val Princeps and Marcus Stone made Surrey cottages immensely popular in later generations. Helen Allingham's rôle in popularising Surrey vernacular was specially significant, though its occupants cannot have appreciated her idealism.

83 *Manor House Lodge, Shere, designed by Edwin Lutyens for Sir Reginald More Bray.*

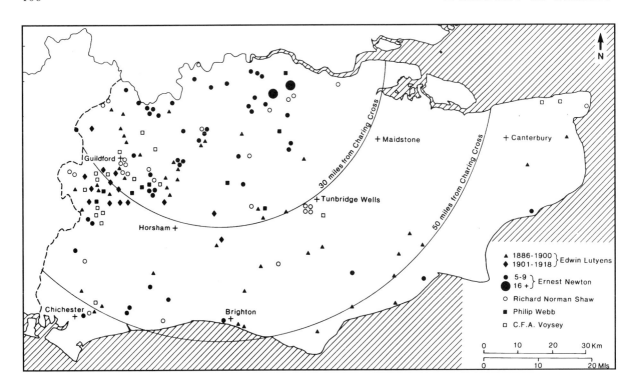

84 *The last country houses in the south east.*

The most inspired creator of the 'Surrey Style' was Edwin Lutyens (1869-1944), the most fashionable country-house architect of his day, who, with Gertrude Jekyll, brought about one of Britain's major contributions to domestic architecture. His boyhood was spent at Thursley amidst many fine old Surrey houses on the verge of the west Surrey heaths and as a young man he met Jekyll at the home of Harry Mangles, at Littleworth, a pioneer in the introduction of the rhododendron. Lutyens' ideas were spread by the intricate networkings of his native society recounted by Jane Brown in *Lutyens and the Edwardians* and by Edward Hudson, founder of *Country Life*, who so greatly shared his vision that he became the promoter of Lutyens' Edwardian dream houses for country living.

The Manor House Lodge at Shere (1894) shows Lutyens' ability to handle local building materials with many joinery details such as wooden pegging with a clever and unusual splayed plan for a small and awkward site. 'Goddards' at Abinger (1908), Lutyens' first symmetrical Arts and Crafts building, has beautifully kept gardens designed by Gertrude Jekyll and is a fine example of Arts and Crafts principles and of the collaboration of Lutyens and Jekyll.

The Guildford district is particularly rich in Arts and Crafts architecture and gardens on account of its ease of access to London. Several of the forerunners of the Arts and Crafts Movement are well represented, including Norman Shaw and Sir Ernest George, whose pupils included Lutyens. C.F.A. Voysey has four major houses, including Greyfriars on the Hog's

Back (originally Sturgis House) above Puttenham. Voysey was an assistant of George Devey, who was a pioneer in the revival of Kentish vernacular. He articulated an approach to life and work based on simple outdoor life and was 'fortunate in finding enough vegetarians and Fabian socialists to keep him in business'. Baillie Scott's prolific career includes three houses on the south side of Guildford, dating to 1910-13.

Many other exceptionally interesting examples of Surrey vernacular exist. They include Great Tangley Manor, one of the finest of old Surrey houses to which Philip Webb made several alterations and additions over 20 years from the late 1880s in an attempt to reproduce the spirit, not the letter, of traditional skills. Vann, below Blackdown, was a group of buildings made into a family home by Arts and Crafts church architect W.D. Caroë whose grandson lives there and carries on the family practice.

Lutyens' first major commission was 'Munstead Wood', near Godalming, built for Gertrude Jekyll (1843-1932) in 1896. In the work of this artist and gardener the influence of her west Surrey 'spirit of place' is even stronger than in Lutyens. She lived her long life at Bramley and Munstead amongst the exceptionally variegated landscape of heaths, woods, orchards and river meadows. It was a veritable 'wild garden' of a landscape thanks to its geological diversity and was aptly likened by her to a 'cosmic wonderland'. Her home 'Munstead Wood' was regarded as an ideal version of the 'Surrey Style' and brought the Surrey house to a wide public.

She was strongly influenced in her artistic consciousness by J.M.W. Turner, John Ruskin and H.B. Brabazon, and also by the touch of 'careless freedom' of the Impressionists. She was also visibly inspired by the old-fashioned Surrey cottage gardens crowded with informally grouped hardy plants. Such gardens were becoming better known in England through the medium of Helen Allingham's and Birket Foster's watercolours. To Gertrude Jekyll, naturally arranged groups of plants as in the wild and in cottage gardens were a form of gardening translated into terms of painting:

85 *Lutyens' Tigbourne, Witley.*

'planting gardens is like painting the landscape with living things'. The cottage gardens and her familiar Surrey wildscape are both closely mirrored in her garden designs and with an artist's eye she drew greatly upon them, in particular for her teaching of sympathetic colour planning and grouping.

Another strong influence on Gertrude Jekyll was William Robinson (1838-1935), of Gravetye, Sussex, the author of *The Wild Garden* (1870) and innumerable works on landscape gardening and forestry, whose uncommon energy touched every aspect of arranging

86 *Edwin Lutyens.*

plants in bold, natural groupings. Her partnership with Edwin Lutyens, her many contributions to *The Garden* (edited by William Robinson), and her many books spread her garden prescriptions across the face of England. The summit of her achievement was the collaboration with Lutyens. Between them they devised 27 gardens between 1890 and 1900 and a further 30 in the following decade for Lutyens' revivalist houses, and in all Miss Jekyll undertook over 300 gardening commissions.

Another contemporary landscape contribution to Surrey was the planting up of barren land with trees and the display of the vast reservoirs of hardy exotics brought back by collectors from the cool and temperate parts of the world. Surrey is particularly associated with this establishment of arboreta and pineta. G.F. Wilson began his famous Wisley Garden (now the Royal Horticultural Society's) in 1878. Like many of the new gardeners, he was a wealthy merchant, a candle manufacturer by trade, one of the many important businessmen in Surrey. He chose a wild and sandy spot and created a magnificent tree collection. His passion for arboreta spread like wildfire in west Surrey where the acid, sandy soils were highly suitable. The making of the Winkworth arboretum (now owned by the National Trust) by Dr. Wilfrid Fox after the Second World War marks the end of an era. Landowners had become more and more fascinated by species of rhododendron and azalea and one can still recapture something of the excitement by which Surrey plant collectors examined and discussed each new collection of seeds brought back from remote and previously unvisited parts of South-East Asia, China and Japan by such adventurous plant hunters as E.H. Wilson, George Forest and Frank Kingdon-Ward. Fittingly, such Surrey landscapes of the Age of Empire close some 300 years of landscape making. It is strange that man's latest chapter in Surrey has been shaped in Nature's first beginnings.

87 *Clayton Adams' rendering of the Surrey 'Wild' in 1885. Adams had a studio on Coneyhurst Hill, Ewhurst which provided him with an eyrie overlooking the Wealds of Surrey and Sussex. His landscapes epitomise the new outlook on nature as a restorative for jaded urban-dwellers that is associated with Victorians' sense of an increasing separation from their natural environment.*

16

The Old Rural Society (1840-1918)

With Gertrude Jekyll's delightful *Old West Surrey* (1904) we can in imagination recall the contemporary Surrey country people and their ways of life. Cottages and little farms still survived with the traditional bacon loft built into the great living room chimney (where the flitches were stored until they were deliciously smoked). About the broad firesides (adapted to wood-burning) were handsome chimney cranes on which pots were suspended over the fire, cast-iron fire-dogs and chimney backs. Older folk still treasured their heavy oak furniture—tables, forms, dressers, and large oaken 'linen-hutches' on the bare floors of the upstairs rooms, and four-poster beds with spotless hangings and lavender-scented sheets. In stone-floored kitchens and cider cellars, well-scoured wooden trenchers, old stoneware and leather harvest bottles lined the shelves of white elm dressers. A rose-trained porch led into the flower-borders giving off the scent of lupins, stocks, wallflowers, heartsease, and several sweet-smelling shrubs and herbs. In the kitchen garden, shading pig-sty and hen-roost, were sturdy fruit-trees of the old-fashioned variety such as ribstone and golden-pippin, Blenheim orange, codling, russet, as well as cherry, and possibly also medlar and quince. A portable cider press was kept. Apple wassailing took place on Twelfth Night when the oldest member of the family poured cider over the roots of one of the trees and wedged cider-soaked bread or cake into forks of the branches as a fertility rite.

88   *Gertrude Jekyll.*

Numerous examples still survive of the old Surrey farmhouses and cottages with their traditional barns. The typical Surrey cottage in the 18th century outside the 'stone' district of west Surrey was weather-boarded on the ground floor and provided with a tile-hung upper storey and tile roof. The weather-boarding was not original, but added when beams shrank and let in draughts and rain. Some were entirely built of timber, painted white in local fashion, for example 'Red Lodge' and Manor Farm at Claygate. Barns were built of timber, tarred for weather protection, and were often of large size, seven or eight bays in length, with oak piers and pantile roofs.

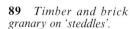

89   *Timber and brick granary on 'steddles'.*

In stone districts more substantial buildings exist. The 'tithe' barns in Witley and Shalford have been converted into houses with the minimum of alteration. The former is a huge building of six bays with an aisle running the full length of the west side. At Shalford a group of former agricultural buildings—'tithe' barn, cow byre, cowman's and shepherd's cottages—has

also been adapted to modern residences in an imaginative and sympathetic manner. The great stone barn at Oxenford Grange, Elstead, on an estate owned by the Cistercians of Waverley before the Dissolution, was designed by the famous revivalist architect, Augustus Pugin, *c*.1840, in the 13th-century style of the great barns still surviving at Beaulieu in the New Forest and at Great Coxwell near Lechlade. It is the finest re-creation of the medieval scene in Surrey, a beautiful, and even moving, vision of the past.

Water-mills were often large wooden structures of great beauty such as Newark Mill, near Ripley (destroyed by fire), or Castle Mill, Dorking. Haybarns were constructed on rat-proof stone piers ('steddles'), and half-timbered, 'brick-nogged' granaries were also similarly constructed. In the Weald a stone causeway would run from the road up to the door of the farmhouse, because in wet weather the path was almost impassable. Wealden farms and cottages were normally roofed in the flaggy varieties of Horsham Stone. These heavy slabs, delightfully mellowed by weathering and moss, are so durable that many existing buildings still retain their original roofing, as is indicated by a liberal amount of soot on its underside. Many of the more substantial half-timbered and stone-roofed farmhouses, picturesque with their fine gables, oriel windows, porches, and vestiges of moats, were bought at the end of the 19th century by London merchants and professional people who converted them into 'gentlemen's residences'. Thus by the Edwardian period it was very rare for one of the accessible oak and stone-roofed farmhouses of Surrey to be still occupied by a farmer who farmed the attached land.

90 *Timber granary on 'steddles'.*

One of the anciently-established rhythms of Surrey country life was the seasonal migration of the poor as hired harvest hands to the Sussex cornlands or to the Farnham and Kent hop fields. This custom was facilitated by the unusual prolongation of the harvest in South-East England because of the variegated soil types and consequently wide range of crops, each with their differing ripening periods. Consequently a casual labourer could follow the regional harvests. The hay harvest of outer London was the earliest. Then followed the corn harvest of the Isle of Wight and the Sussex Coastal Plain, which was followed by that of fruit and hops. In winter there was coppice work. As in the Sussex Weald, this migratory custom was probably well established by the late 14th century. For generations the practice resolved the real difficulty for the large landed estate of the seasonal mobility of labour. By the 18th and 19th centuries it is well documented, none better than in Sturt's ('George Bourne's') writings. In his day the hired helpers walked in bands all night in readiness for the start of work soon after sunrise. For several weeks the hired bands would sleep in barns or out in the open, and then made a jolly journey back with their hard-earned fortune.

The traditional sources of harvest labour in Surrey were the areas of large cottage-bounded commons. The heath parishes around Farnham were half-emptied of able-bodied men in summer. The cottagers, many of them 'squatters' with no legal title to land, cut fern to provide litter for their pigs and cattle, and grew a little wheat in their gardens which was ground at the local mills and baked in bread-ovens heated with furze. These people were

called 'broom squires'. S. Baring-Gould's *The Broom-Squires* (1896), a topographical novel with a setting near Hindhead in the late 18th century, is a reminder of the time when it was a wild region with scattered dwellings along the streams with little hedged gardens and bright green meadows forming small islands amidst the sea of fern and heather. These small 'waste edge' colonies still retain much of their outward aspect though little of the former social atmosphere is retained. 'Broom squires' were not wedded to the place they inhabited, as Sturt noted, and only stayed if the heath gave them a chance of getting food and shelter. In bad winters such as those of 1878-9 and 1889-90 these people suffered great hardship when their chief crops failed, even to the extent of living on the verge of starvation.

91 *The revival of 'merrie England' at Oxenford Grange by Augustus Pugin.*

The small tenant farmers of the Surrey Weald were also in great difficulties at this time on account of the import of cheap corn from overseas. Since the 1780s their fate has been chequered. The 'boom' war economy based on high corn prices collapsed in 1820 with a return to normal peacetime trading. The Surrey labourers' standard of living had improved during that time. Cottages were better furnished than formerly and cottagers lived better, notably consuming more bacon, wheaten bread, tea, coffee and sugar. Between 1820 and the 1840s the labourers and small farmers were severely depressed. Farmers paid off labourers and Wealden parishes became eaten up with the poor. Poor rates rose to unprecedented levels, in some

92 *A charcoal-burner's hut in west Surrey.*

cases as much as four times the annual rent of the land. In the 1830s it was difficult to find tenants for Wealden farms and some landlords were obliged to advance money to tenants to enable them to take land. The soil required so much labour to put into readiness for a crop that in some years the expense of cultivation exceeded the return. In these conditions much land was taken out of cultivation and allowed to tumble to grass. The general fall in corn prices was exacerbated in the Weald by successive wet seasons in the 1870s which caused outbreaks of foot-rot in sheep and prevented the customary fallowing indispensable for cereals.

Some of the most sensitive and observant pictures of Surrey country life ever penned were written by Denham Jordan under the pseudonym of 'Son of the marshes'. The little that is known of his career has to be extracted from the tantalising brief autobiographical details he permits himself in books on natural history of the Weald published between 1889 and 1898. His childhood was spent on the marshes of the Swale in north Kent. He travelled to the United States, but he had a deep familiarity with Surrey and Wealden Sussex. When he was recording his memoirs (edited, and possibly written, by Mrs. Owen Visgar, 'J.A. Owen') he was earning a living as a painter and decorator in Dorking, where he died in 1920. He wrote in the tradition of Richard Jefferies, W.H. Hudson and Edward Thomas, and although much less well known than these writers he can match, and indeed excel, them in the shrewdness of his observations and the charm of his style.

Jordan's great love was the wild country of fir and heather around Dorking, the great heaths on the Hampshire border, or the forested country of the deep Weald. In his walks into the latter he delineates with great clarity the woodlanders and their simple ways of life. They rose before sunrise, and the cycle of tree-felling, copse-cutting, hoop-shaving, hurdle-making, charcoal burning, and bark-stripping kept them employed all year, in contrast to farmhands in corn districts who were generally laid off for part of the winter. They often travelled eight miles a day to and from their place of work and when work necessitated a longer stay they camped out in 'forest' style by making a shanty thatched with fern and provided with a wattle door packed with heather.

As late as the 1880s the remoter parts of Surrey retained, as far at least as outward appearances went, their aspect and ways of life of centuries ago. People often still paid for services in kind: the village shoemaker would take payment in farm produce, for example. Stocks still stood on

village greens; each farm still possessed a limekiln. Communities yet retained some individual characteristics and dialects peculiar to themselves
and were moulded by their different environments as much as they moulded
them. Thus the Surrey Wealdsman was slow of speech (though his wits
were keen). His movements were also rather slow and ponderous, but his
long stride and perfect balance enabled him to cover wet, slippery clays
with agility. Generally, Weald folk were sturdy, well-built people because
puny persons could not have done their work. The men of the heaths (the
fir and heather districts), such as the fern-cutters and stone-diggers, tended
to keep themselves apart from the woodlanders, as did also those of the
wortlebury (hurt) woods near Peaslake. These latter were particularly un-
communicative people addicted to smuggling and other illegal activities
and were taught from childhood 'to see everything but to say nothing'.

93 *Timber-frame of charcoal burner's sleeping hut (after J.R. Armstrong, Open Air Museum, Singleton).*

The works of George Sturt ('George Bourne') of Farnham, who took
over the management of his father's wheelwright's business in 1884 are
masterpieces of recording 19th-century social change in Surrey. His
Bettesworth Book (1901) and *Memoirs of a Surrey Labourer* (1907) were
followed by *Change in the Village* (1912) and *The Wheelwright's Shop*
(1923). It is through Sturt's perceptive understanding of the rapidly-changing
rural civilisation of his timesthat we know something of the nature of
traditional Surrey craftsmanship. The 'rotarius' returned in an occasional
Surrey Poll Tax Return of 1379 is usually the first recorded reference to the
wheelwright trade. The craft of wheel-maker, like that of charcoal burner,
was often handed down from father to son for generations. Sturt's chroni-
cle of the working lives of individual craftsmen is moving and enlightening
and it is skilfully interwoven to show their share in the advancement of
what was then the little town of Farnham. 'In farm wagon or dung-cart,
barley-roller, plough, water-barrel, or what not, the dimensions we chose,
the curves we followed ... were imposed upon us by the nature of the soil
in this or that farm, the temper of this or that customer, or his choice
perhaps in horseflesh.'

Sturt also chronicled perceptively the blotting out of the old cottage
economy on Surrey heaths and Weald. In *Change in the Village* (1912) he
called the old Surrey way of life as 'nothing less than a form of civilization—the home-made civilization of the rural English'. He deemed the
main catalyst of its disintegration to be the enclosure of the commons
which rendered village life 'devoid of hope and interest'. His gardener and
odd-job man, Frederick Grover, the hero of *Bettesworth Book*, personified
the Surrey agricultural labourer to him. Sturt's advocacy of 'folk' industry
with its intimate knowledge of environment and craftsmanship in a society
less acquisitive and aggressive than our own may yet have a place in the
world of the future.

17

The Surrey Side of London (1800-1914)

94 *Lambeth water-front (1886).*

By the early 18th century Surrey nearest to London had become a great purveyor to the metropolis. 'Dorking' fowls from the Wealden smallholders; delicious, sweet 'Banstead' mutton, fattened on all the farms within a 20-mile radius of the City; vegetables from the market-gardens of Battersea and Lambeth; fresh milk from hundreds of cow-keepers in Camberwell, Peckham, Brixton and beyond; and immense quantities of pigs fed on the waste from the riverside starch factories and corn distilleries; all this food poured into the London wholesale markets. It was not until late Georgian times that the insatiable demand for building sites within the capital began to drive out the Surrey market-gardeners and cow-keepers. The first stage of this invasion is marked by the building of Westminster Bridge in 1750 and its new approach roads leading to Dover, Brighton and Portsmouth, such as the 'Wash way' across Lambeth Marsh which led to the Brixton Causeway, also on low-lying ground. These were the great coaching arteries along which houses first slowly crept in the 1780s and then were to envelop completely the ancient tightly-clustered and well-filled villages of Camberwell, Peckham, Stockwell, Streatham and Clapham. Rocque's map of 1762 is a fine rendering of this phase. For the next two generations, the advance of building was gradual and piecemeal. Coach travellers in the 1790s still glimpsed fine villas such as 'Grove Hill', Camberwell, or 'Loughborough House', in Brixton, amidst market gardens backed by the gently-rising wooded hills of Norwood. 'Grove Hill' was for 40 years one of the most famous sights on the Brighton road.

London was the first world capital to have grown so hugely and rapidly. In terms of physical growth London expanded from the 8.5 square miles on John Rocque's 1746 map, to about 22 square miles on the 1822 map of John Cary and rose to some 50 square miles in 1851 and then continuously to 120 square miles in 1901 and to over 200 square miles in 1939. About one half of this enormous metropolis was built across Surrey farmland.

An early stage in the growth of London south of the Thames was the enclosure of the common lands in the manor of Lambeth in 1806. This met with fierce resistance. The commons were of great recreational value to the citizens of London and Westminster across the Thames. It was also argued

114

that drovers supplying the London markets would be deprived of essential resting-places for their livestock. In short, the commons of this corner of Surrey had long been an essential part of London life. Nevertheless, the Enclosure Award allotted Norwood and Kennington Commons into plots suitable for building. As late as this time, as Horwood's fine map of 1799 demonstrates, Kennington marked the end of built-up London, and even in 1824 the Oval was the furthest limit of houses.

By the 1840s a full-scale invasion was in progress. The advance of London's railways had much to do with this. In 1838 the Southampton Railway opened its Nine Elms depot bringing rapid industrialisation. Westwards the railway station at Putney led to residential development along the Upper and Lower Richmond Roads by the 1840s, later to be joined by development at Putney Hill and Heath.

By the 1840s the great mid-century economic expansion was leading to the creation of commercial and governmental offices, of docks and ware-housing and the advance of railway lines, stations and goods yards. The railways displaced great numbers of people who were housed further out. The construction of the railway line from Nine Elms deeper into London at Waterloo involved the demolition of about 700 houses and that from

95 *Norwood, before the population explosion through migration outwards from London into the nearby countryside which created Croydon, formerly isolated from the capital, into a city in all but name. South Norwood had appeared following enclosure of common-lands in 1808 with the construction of the Surrey Canal and the opening of the railway to Brighton. Upper Norwood came into being as a residential area later.*

96 *An example of Lambeth stoneware by Louisa E. Edwards of Doulton's, 1877.*

97 *The extending railway network up to 1914.*

London Bridge to Charing Cross and Cannon Street also removed many hundreds of the poor. In all some 24,000 persons were 'dishoused' in South London by railway construction between 1840 and the 1860s. One of the last of the schemes was the LCDR Metropolitan expansion of 1862-4 with its four miles of viaducts, 346 arches and 24 wrought-iron bridges, bringing over-crowding and distress in the wake of demolition.

By the 1860s Thames-side working-class or artisan sectors had arisen in Bermondsey and Lambeth and dockyard and wharfage extensions were marked at Rotherhithe. Here rookeries became still more overcrowded, the maze of alleys and byways desperately overcrowded with the poor. Meanwhile, the suburban frontiers had engulfed Tulse Hill, Camberwell, Peckham, Dulwich, Clapham, Streatham. Cheap terraces became slums almost as soon as they were built but the cheap rents and easy walking distance to central London ensured a ready supply of tenants, many of them women out-workers and Bermondsey leather-workers, lightermen, watermen and printers. Areas such as Newington or Walworth had originally housed clerks and artisans earlier in the century but by the 1870s were overcrowded with casual and low-paid workers 'dishoused' from central London. A smart villa district

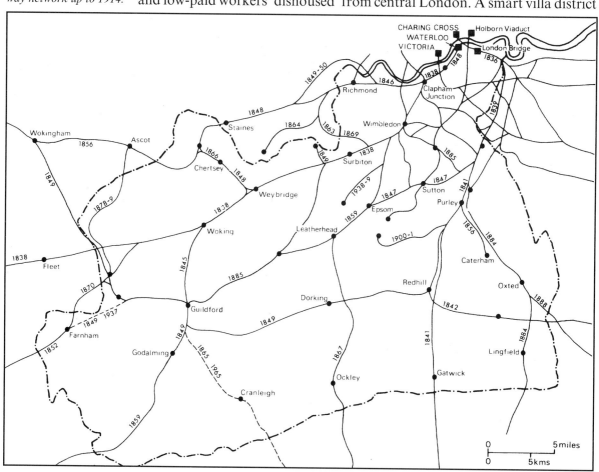

grew up at Clapham Park over dairying and market-gardening countryside in what the developers hoped to form 'A sort of southern Belgravia, though on a humbler scale'. Despite all the development Clapham Common still had 'an air of rusticity' as late as the 1890s and mounted concerts with its Philharmonic Society and string quartets, lectures and readings.

On Thames-side the social and economic differences were both enormous and growing because palaces and the worst London slums were cheek by jowl. One of London's worst rookeries was the fever-den, devil's acre or slum of Jacob Island south of Bermondsey Wall, Dickens's grim setting for the pursuit and death of Bill Sykes in *Oliver Twist*. The vice, poverty and over-crowding in St Saviour's, Southwark almost matched it.

In Brixton the pavements crept further and further from London. Loughborough House ended its days as a finishing school for the 'sons of gentlemen' before being demolished in 1853 to make way for more than 70 houses built in 1854-5. In Loughborough Road the ground landlord specified houses 'not inferior to third rate'; 'fourth rate' houses as defined by the current Metropolitan Building Act being built in side streets. Few of the present inhabitants of Brixton today have the means of living in Victorian third- and fourth-raters. A 'third-rate house' was a rather splendidly dignified semi-detached residence with a minimum of six large rooms; these are now being modernised and let as two or even more tenements. The 'fourth-rate' houses are tending to be replaced by modern flats. A little earlier than the Loughborough district 'an immense quantity of new building' sprang up in north Brixton at Angell Town where its new district church was begun in 1845.

By the 1840s it was obvious to William Farr and later to Dickens and George Godwin that street clearances of slum areas merely aggravated and transferred the problem of the poor from one parish to the next. Greenwood's *Night in a Workhouse* (1866) and Sims' *How the Poor Live* (1889), based on actual experience at Lambeth and Southwark respectively, first brought home to comfortably off readers the physical and moral degradation of the urban poor in Surrey.

It is, however, from Charles Booth's *Life and labour of the people of London* that we obtain the most accurate and vivid descriptions of social life in the streets converging towards the Elephant and Castle, the hub of the new South London. His elaborately annotated maps show the wide highroads coloured bright red to signify well-to-do middle-class inhabitants or small shopkeepers, and in imagination we can visualise these roads crammed with the new clanging trams jostling with horse-drawn omnibuses and cabs. The poorer streets ran off these carriage roads and as the oldest inhabited areas nearest the river bank were reached they degenerated into dark, noisome alleys and nests of courts. When people 'got a bit decent' they rented a house in Clapham or Sydenham; the less successful remained. Although the great riverside belt of the south bank was uniformly characterised by the poverty and squalor grimly manifested in the streets, its local life was based on a number of distinct communities which kept blazingly alive the strong loyalties of a village. The Borough High Street and its vicinity, including Tabard Street, was famous for its inns—over 200 of them—the relic of the coaching days when travellers entering and leaving London by the Old Kent Road took lodgings there. Here, too, lived the Billingsgate porters, extraordinary bundles of human energy, who ran to and from the ships and railway vans, and many hundreds of costermongers who supplied in street markets most of the wants of the poor. Further east, Bermondsey was the home of leather-workers and tanners. Rotherhithe had its ship-chandlers about the docks, its fish-curers and basket-makers and a great colony of Irish stevedores, orderly and hard-working by day, but rolling drunk in the streets by night, brawling and going about in hooligan gangs. Between Blackfriars Bridge and Lambeth Palace, in the shadow of the great railway stations, lived an army of cabmen and 'costers', not all as picturesque as the pearly-buttoned and be-plumed costers of story and song, for some were so poor that they carried their own wares, being unable to afford either donkey or barrow. South again one encountered the Lambeth potteries and food factories where in a single street the air was charged with the delicious vapours of strawberry jam mixed with the stench of boiling fat, tannin and vinegar. Here the highway of the Thames, crowded with the merchandise of the whole world shipped up its river, and plied by innumerable 'penny' steamers, was lined by the shabbiest, blackest and ugliest buildings imaginable, chiefly decayed and ruinous warehouses that had lost their trade to the docks downstream.

Meanwhile, outer suburbs were being created by the London and Southampton Railway which opened its first line between Nine Elms and Woking in 1838, with trains to Southampton in 1840 and its extension to Waterloo in 1848 on a viaduct of 235 arches. Similarly the London to

98 *Fore Street, Lambeth led to the Archbishop's Palace and his lucrative crossing place at Horse Ferry Dock before the construction of Westminster Bridge. The slum street was swept away with the building of Bazalgette's Albert Embankment in the late 1960s.*

Brighton and South Coast Railway extended to London Bridge and Victoria and the South-Eastern Railway had terminuses at Charing Cross and Cannon Street. The railway companies themselves promoted housing development on their routes. The LSW in 1859 granted a 10 per cent reduction in fares to occupiers of larger houses on Kingston Hill. Railways, however, normally followed rather than initiated new settlement. Croydon was a battleground for the LBSCR and SER from the beginning and by 1876 had no fewer than eight stations with 300 trains daily to and from London. Poorer people tended to move out from the congested areas with workmen's tickets for the railways, from 1865 and cheaper forms of public

99 *Writing from Herne Hill in 1885 John Ruskin in* Praeterita *described his childhood home on a 'once rustic eminence' from 1824. It still retained its leafy seclusion when he wrote: 'I can still walk up and down from the Fox Tavern to Herne Hill railway station imagining I am four years old'. Note the houses arranged in 'partner-couples'. They commanded magnificent views and had formal front gardens set in old evergreens with extensive back gardens. Ruskin was later horrified by the adverse changes.*

transport such as horse-drawn trams. By 1906 the London United Tramways Company was operating an electric tram service to Kingston-upon-Thames and Surbiton, extending to Merton in 1907 and by 1915 an efficient service of trams ran from Westminster to Tooting. This improvement in public transport led to housing development at Wimbledon, Raynes Park and between Balham and Tooting and along the railway at Wallington, Carshalton, Sutton, Cheam, Cousldon and Purley. At Mitcham and New Malden the population almost doubled between 1901 and 1911 and rose enormously at Merton and Morden.

Changes from the Housing of the Working Classes Act of 1890 were dramatic. This gave local authorities the power to acquire land compulsorily for additional houses, extending by 1900 even beyond their boundaries. About 20 London authorities adopted the Act. The most extensive use was that of the London County Council at Tooting and Norbury. Between 1903 and 1911 the Totterdown village estate at Tooting had 1,300 new houses. The first LCC 'out-county' estate was built at Norbury between 1906 and 1910.

Many must have witnessed with anguish the blotting out of the lovely south bank countryside. One who has written sadly of this experience is John Ruskin (1819-1900), one of the most widely read and admired of all Victorian writers on the art of the human environment. His father's practice was to take summer lodgings for his family in Dulwich or Hampstead as a change from the air of Brunswick Square, a convention which dates from the early 18th century, as we have seen. In 1824 he bought a new villa on the top of Herne Hill, one of only two pairs of houses existing there. This again was typical of development in South London at this time. 'The main army', said a contemporary, 'is preceded by an advance of villas ...

seizing a few picked positions. Then come the more solid ranks of the semi-detached ... along the high roads and in the neighbourhood of railway stations.' As Ruskin grew older he witnessed the streams and meadow ditches of his youth putridly bricked-over, the ponds drained, the hedge-rows and copses grubbed up and burned, the farmhouses demolished. As the local railway stations were opened the new railways brought hordes of 'expiating roughs' by every excursion train to view the Crystal Palace. The 'politely inhabited groves' of which he writes in his autobiography *Præterita* were the haunts of well-to-do London tradesmen, usually possessing 'a great cortège of footmen and glitter of plate, extensive pleasure grounds, costly hot-houses and carriages driven by coachmen in wigs', and whose ladies dashed up to doors in a barouche. Down the hill were the small shopkeepers of the Walworth Road, and behind them were the houses of the poor towards the Thames, unseen by the counting-house clerks who daily took the horse-drawn omnibus into the self-satisfied City of the late 19th century.

Meanwhile, the suburbs further from London were developing. The effects of railway construction on the location of new housing estates in the vicinity of Kingston-upon-Thames is particularly interesting. The old borough of Kingston opposed the building of the Nine Elms and Woking railway (later extended to Southampton) in the interest of its coaching trade. The railway line was built instead in 1838 through Surbiton, in a remote corner of Kingston parish, and then almost entirely rural. The first station was named 'Kingston', though it was three miles away from the town. From a small estate by the station Surbiton rapidly grew to a

100 *P. Gustave Doré's sardonic bird's eye view from the steam railways threading through South London from Charing Cross, London Bridge, Cannon Street and Waterloo, threading through interminable working-class terraces, potteries and workyards crammed between the viaducts (1872).*

population of 15,000 by 1901 and in the manner of a 'high-class' suburb was plentifully endowed with large Gothic churches and good shops. Shortly afterwards New Malden (to distinguish it from the old agricultural settlement nearby) mushroomed around Christ Church, built in 1866. This town was never served by express trains, and consequently residential property tended to be of a cheaper variety. Kingston Hill came on to the building market in the 1850s and new villas sprang up when Norbiton station was opened in 1863. In 1878 this 'smart' estate erected its own church (St Paul's), a common practice of the time, although the parish church of St Peter's, Norbiton, was very close.

A further stage in urbanisation was reached when villages further from London were 'developed' when the 'New Line' from London to

101 *Montague Close, Southwark, expressed in the mid-19th century the harsh work-a-day world of the old Surrey waterside.*

Guildford via Leatherhead was opened in 1885. Claygate and Oxshott (on attractive heathland) then spread around their respective stations. By the 1880s many of the middle-class Londoners either could not afford, or felt submerged rather than freed in the new but somewhat anonymous inner south-west and north London, and they therefore acquired a partiality for suburban life. This process, with the help of the railways, evolved the more exclusive outer suburb with its villa residences, fast-growing lengths of laurel and *laurustinus* extending over the countryside. This soon attracted considerable literary attention. H.G. Wells's *Ann Veronica* (1909) cuttingly refers to a stuffiness and air of conscious elegance of Worcester Park.

These examples of urban growth show the scale of the ever-increasing tide of building, so furious and long-lasting that by 1900 the built-up edge of London stood 10 to 12 miles across Surrey from the Thames. Esher Green was then almost the first strip of 'countryside' glimpsed by travellers on the Southampton Railway and the Surrey side of London had become a great suburban continent, part of the largest urban concentration which the world had yet seen. 'Unspoilt' Surrey became a mecca for the urbanised population of its fringes.

18

The Surrey Towns

Surrey shares with its neighbouring counties an inheritance of old towns built to a scale appropriate to its landscape and filled with gracefully proportioned houses so carefully preserved that they have retained much of their old identity and character. Indeed, most of the old Surrey towns possess the quality which Thomas Sharp in *English Panorama* has said: 'We in England once showed a natural genius—the genius of creating towns that nearly always have had pleasantness and seemliness; that often have quite remarkable beauty; that always have maintained a comfortable human scale'. Two of the towns sited in the classic gaps through the Chalk escarpment of the North Downs—Farnham and Guildford—have townscapes of an architectural quality that places them amongst the finest English country towns and they are matched by the unspoilt parts of Richmond-upon-Thames, a town of quite a different origin, and by the lesser towns of Godalming and Haslemere. In few parts of England is it still possible to savour so much of Georgian beauty and refinement. These

102 *Guildford—the High Street still retains much of its traditional charm and Aylward's clock remains in its prominent position.*

townscapes vividly demonstrate the cleavage between Victorian and earlier Surrey. It is impossible to explain why these towns are such remarkably unspoilt expressions of the pre-railway age without exploring their origins and development, and also of such rivals as Redhill, Hindhead and Woking, new towns constructed with the coming of the railways, when the pattern of human existence in Surrey was changing so rapidly. The lack of 19th-century industrial development in Surrey also needs to be borne in mind.

Before the Census Returns, beginning in 1801, there is little in the way of accurate statistics of the urban population, but a reasonably satisfactory ranking of Surrey towns can

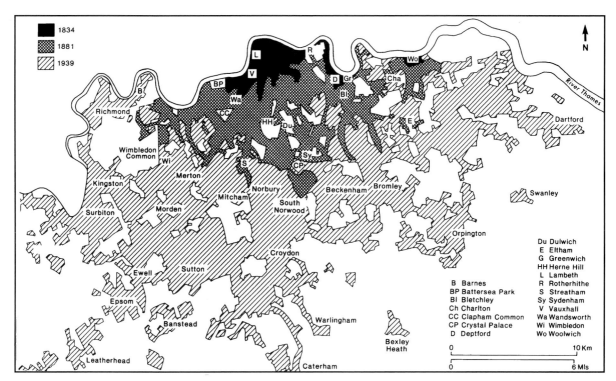

103 *The growth of south London, c.1834-1939.*

be based on the assessments for Hearth Tax in the 1660s which provide information as to the number of houses, and hence, in some measure, of population. On this basis Guildford and Kingston-upon-Thames were in the first rank of Surrey's market towns, each comprising about 500 houses. Farnham, with about 300 dwellings, came next in size. Croydon, Godalming and Reigate had an intermediate position in the county with about 160-180 houses each. Epsom, Dorking and Leatherhead were small towns in the class of only 100-120 houses, whilst Haslemere with about 80 houses was really an urban village, although sending two members to the unreformed Parliament. These market towns were all eclipsed in size by the large concentrations of population on the Surrey banks of the Thames. Bermondsey in the 1660s, for example, consisted of 800 densely-packed dwellings, many occupied by people so poor that they were exempted from taxation.

Although **Epsom** had long been supplanted as a spa by the late 18th century, it continued to thrive as a resort for London merchants and gentry intent on racing and hunting. Numerous country seats existed on the fringes of the town, several of which are particularly rewarding places to visit. **Dorking** gained in some respects from the building of the London to Brighton turnpike, but lost in others. The London gentry 'discovered' the beauty of its local scenery and in summer took up residence in the town, dining on the freshwater fish and poultry for which the town had long been renowned. Although residentially the town prospered, its corn and cattle markets declined in favour of Horsham, also on the London to Brighton turnpike, and better placed for the collection of Low Weald produce. This commercial setback probably explains the report of its 'old, ill-built and badly paved' appearance by a writer in the *Gentleman's Magazine* in 1787. Unrejuvenated by the railway until the late 19th century (Dorking had no direct connection with London until 1867) the decayed old town was then largely rebuilt by the generation witnessing the rise of Woodyer's splendid new parish church (1868-77), dominating the wide streets and setting the theme for the entire town.

Leatherhead is one of many English places provided with the essentials of a medieval town, in this case, four streets meeting in a market-place at the cross-roads, which nevertheless failed to grow beyond the scale of a village until modern times. One of the main reasons for Leatherhead's past smallness was the difficulty of road communication through the Mole valley in winter. Not until the coaching era did Leatherhead become a 'gap' town commanding a major route to the coast through the Vale of Mickleham. In 1821, the Rev. James Dallaway remarked that the village 'is losing its primary character and converting itself by a multiplication of inconsiderable houses into an appendage of the enormous London ...'. So much of Leatherhead bore the marks of obsolescence in the newcomers' eyes that even by Dallaway's day almost all the old buildings had been demolished.

Farnham is a beautiful little town which has kept much of its identity as an old market and coaching town, living on the products of its local countryside and keeping busy its corn and hop merchants, drovers and wheelwrights. Its history in the 18th century was not one of decline, as at Dorking, but of rising prosperity, with a corn market described by Defoe in 1722 as the greatest in England outside London. This is reflected in its different

104 *The stone stairway to the Keep at Farnham Castle.*

townscape which has been preserved by a remarkable exercise in voluntary effort. We can still enjoy the visual delight of a Georgian townscape described by Christopher Hussey and Nigel Temple as the best in England.

Farnham is a typical example of a town organically evolving through time within a country setting. The roofs of medieval Farnham covered barns and little farmsteads along its single street below the Bishop of Winchester's castle commanding the easiest route between Southampton and London. From early times a cloth town, then prominent as a corn market, the culture of hops, begun at the end of the 16th century, came to provide most of the wealth of the town. Hops were grown on the former common fields lying on the narrow strip, only a few hundred yards wide, marked by the Upper Greensand outcrop. Not until the 1860s did Farnham expand and disperse the hop growers along the whole length of this exposure at the foot at the Hog's Back. Hops became the *raison d'être* of Farnham to the extent that hop kilns were built in its streets, business people shut up their shops for a week at drying time, and the quick-set hedges and belts of trees erected to shelter the hops from the wind gave added beauty to its countryside. The splendid façades of warm brick, classically door-cased houses, in Castle Street and the many little yards attached to the smaller houses in East and West Streets constitute one of the most distinguished townscapes in Surrey.

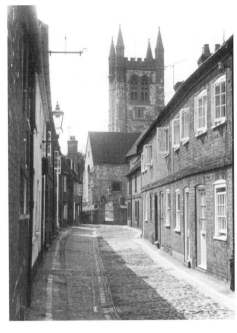

105 *Farnham still wears the air of a small country town. These cottages are heavily-disguised timber-framed dwellings.*

Although a jewel of Georgian building, the greatest buildings in Farnham are the castle and palace of the Prince Bishops of Winchester which have been lived in almost continuously for 800 years. The oldest part of the castle is the keep erected about 1138 by Bishop Henry de Blois, a grandson of William the Conqueror and a younger brother of King Stephen. The Great Hall and Norman Chapel date from about 1180. To the 13th century are attributed the kitchen, the Bishop's Camera (drawing room), the spiral stairs leading up to it, and the Gate House. The outer wall of stone was built in the 14th century. Later alterations include the remarkably early red-brick tower gateway of Bishop William of Wayneflete (1447-86). The present hall of the palace is essentially the Norman Great Hall remodelled by Bishop George Morley in the late 17th century. Stained glass in the windows inserted by Bishop Thorold (1890-5) includes the arms of the nine bishops of Winchester who became Chancellors of England.

We have already traced the history of **Guildford** to the mid-16th century. The town by then had greatly declined from its medieval importance. John Speed remarked in 1611 that 'it had been far greater than now it is when the palace of our English kings was therein set'. A further cause of impoverishment was the decline of the woollen industry which led George Abbot, Archbishop of Canterbury and native of Guildford, to endow in 1619 the Hospital of the Blessed Trinity to alleviate the town's distress. This fine brick building, reminiscent of an early Tudor gatehouse, still survives with little alteration. A further vivid reminder of Guildford's decline is the beautifully-made plan of the town by Matthew Richardson in 1739, depicting the little town still bounded by its Saxon and medieval

106 *Abbot's Hospital at Guildford survives as one of the finest examples of Jacobean architecture. It was endowed by Archbishop Abbot, a native of the town, in an attempt to alleviate the widespread poverty which had resulted from the decline of the Surrey cloth trade.*

defences. Little change had probably occurred in the cramped nature of the town's site for over 500 years.

In the second half of the 17th century, however, there are signs of a rejuvenation at Guildford. The outstanding event was the construction of the river Wey Navigation, opened in 1653 on the initiative of Sir Richard Weston of Sutton Place, who brought from Holland the idea of artificially controlling water in a working river by locks. One of the citizens of Guildford most closely connected with this scheme was Richard Scotcher. He was an important dyer and clothier with a 'pumpe' in Castle Street (probably a device for pumping water from an artesian well). He is one of the few clothiers once making the excellent Guildford blue cloth whose names have come down to us. Scotcher himself was driven into bankruptcy by the mismanaged Wey Navigation but it brought lasting benefit to Guildford as a means of cheap and effective transport of bulk goods such as grain, timber and building materials. The greatest source of trouble to the owners of the Wey Navigation were the millers along the river. For nearly two centuries it was their habit to draw off so much water into their mill ponds that some grain barges could not get through the locks and owners were obliged to have corn ground at their mills. A great treadmill crane on Guildford Wharf, a memento of this long era of water transport, has been preserved and by the generosity of Harry W. Stevens, the last representative of Guildford's long line of watermen; the banks of the river Wey have been taken into the custody of the National Trust. A further sign of growing prosperity in Guildford in the late 17th century was the rebuilding of the Guildhall in the High Street in 1683. To this is still affixed John Aylward's celebrated clock, provided with a fine new case when the Guildhall was altered, but in fact probably more than a century

107 *Guildford's charm is increased by numerous medieval passageways called gates, some only wide enough for pedestrians, but mostly lined with interesting small shops.*

older. It was given to the Elizabethan town by Aylward who was first refused permission by the Gild Merchant to set up in business in the town as a clockmaker because he was a 'foreigner'.

With the final decay of its cloth industry at the beginning of the 18th century, Guildford increasingly relied for prosperity upon its growing coaching trade to Brighton, Portsmouth and Southampton. The *Angel* inn still retains its rambling yard and stabling, a legacy of its former function as a posting house. Although modern manufacturing industry is now extensive at Guildford the outward appearance of the High Street and its adjacent streets is very little changed from what Matthew

108 *Much business took place at the town wharf. Barges from London unloaded coal and grain and returned laden with timber, beer, and bark for tanning. In 1794 the Town Council levied 1 d. per load handled by the Wey Navigation and raised enough to pave the town streets.*

Richardson saw in 1739. In few parts of the London region does one have a greater sense of a vigorous, living town, a growing organism, which has chosen to regard the past not as an encumbrance, but as an enrichment of the present and an inspiration for the future.

Godalming's prosperity was principally based for centuries on the manufacture and marketing of woollens. This was replaced progressively in the 17th century by its hosiery and knitwear industry introduced from London which, although it became largely concentrated in the East Midlands, survived by specialisation against all the odds. Factories have now been closed but small-scale production by specialised knitwear firms continues.

Richmond-upon-Thames, anciently named Shene from the beauty of its green hill reflected in the shining river, and for long a minor part of the royal manor of Kingston, first came into repute with its choice as a residence by the Plantagenet kings. With the rebuilding of the palace on a magnificent scale around two main courtyards by Henry VII, who renamed the place Richmond after his birthplace and earldom in Yorkshire, Richmond became increasingly a centre of fashion and pleasure during the Tudor dynasty. A delightful painting in the style of the Flemish School of *c.*1629 is evidence that Richmond still retained all the characteristics of a rural village. A century later, as is disclosed in the engraving of 'The Prospect of Richmond' (1726) by H. Overton and J. Hook, Richmond then possessed more of an urban atmosphere, but the Georgians who created Richmond did not intend to make a town but a country retreat and consequently Richmond has none of the noble planning of Bath or Brighton, no wide streets, stately crescents and few of the bow windows and hooded balconies we normally associate with the Regency. Instead Richmond became a fashionable playground for frustrated urban Georgians who left their town

109 Richmond Palace *by Anthony van Wyngaerd (c.1527).*

houses in Mayfair and Leicester Square at the weekend and during the summer. Horace Walpole's correspondence throws much light on this social process that still gives a special air to Richmond's buildings discoverable on one of John Rocque's maps. Under 1789 he writes: 'Richmond is the first request this summer. Mrs. Bouverie is settled there with a large court. The Sheridans are there, too, and the Bunbury's'. Forty years earlier he had remarked upon the new fashion of leaving London at the weekend. 'As I passed over the Green I saw Lord Bath, Lord Londsdale and half-dozen more of the White's Club ... come to Richmond every Saturday and Sunday to play at whist ... [it is now] a fashion to go out of town at the end of the week ...'.

It was in the Georgian period that Richmond enjoyed its greatest fame as a resort. Its Green, its Park (imparked by Charles I in 1637), its unrivalled riverside scenery observable from Richmond Hill, and its accessibility, made it a perfect resort for Londoners. It also enjoyed the consistent and enthusiastic patronage of Hanoverian royalty. Society flocked in its wake and this was a decisive factor in the accelerated building during the later 18th century.

The earliest building at Kew Gardens, Kew House, renamed Kew Palace, was the home of the Capel family and it was Sir Henry Capel who, in the late 17th century, purchased the first trees at Kew. The house dates from 1631 and is typical of the jolly Dutch Renaissance mansions fashionable at that time. With the Hanoverians Kew became part of the royal enclave

XIII *The Harlequin Theatre and the large shopping mall have established Redhill as a major focal point in east Surrey.*

XIV *The British American Tobacco (BAT) office block dominates Woking and Surrey for miles around and overlooks the massive Peacocks Centre, an all-embracing shopping and leisure development which is said to be bigger than any other in Europe. H.G. Wells had Woking in mind when he predicted in* Anticipations *(1900) that the city would diffuse itself over great belts of countryside. In sharp contrast are nearby Wentworth and St George's Hill where W.G. Tarrant built large private houses for wealthy London businessmen which have now acquired celebrity status.*

XV *Kingston's market continues after many hundreds of years with a background largely of mock-Tudor facades and Italianate extravaganza.*

XVI *Edward Wilkins Waite's* The Stackyard *recalls the changed agricultural scene in Surrey which not only has displaced the farmyard, the haystack, duckpond and muck-heap in favour of slurry tanks and ugly grain stores, but is itself being displaced by new settlement, roads and 'horsey-culture'.*

which extended upstream to Richmond. George II lived at Richmond Lodge during his estrangement from his father, and his son, Frederick, lived next door at Kew House with his wife, the Princess Augusta. On Frederick's death the Princess began the major collection of 'exotics' which has ultimately made Kew world famous. She also commissioned the architect, Sir William Chambers, to embellish her grounds with classical and oriental follies, including the 10-storey Pagoda. George II inherited both Richmond Lodge and Kew Palace and combined the grounds and continued the planting. He and Queen Charlotte liked to stay at Kew free of court and with only a small staff of servants. The rooms are furnished in 18th-century style with an endearing collection of Hanoverian bric-à-brac including royal toys and snuffboxes. It was not until Victoria came to the throne that the gardens were given to the nation (1841) and achieved their international reputation under the two great botanists, Sir William Hooker and his son, Sir Joseph. Amidst the many treasures of Kew, is the spectacular Palm House inspired by Paxton's Great Stove at Chatsworth and, contrastingly, Queen Charlotte's private garden with its *cottage ornée*.

Under this royal patronage Richmond became a metropolitan pleasure adjunct, bearing something of the kind of relationship that Versailles did to the 18th-century Paris. Visitors and residents ambled around Richmond Park in their chaises; promenaded on the Green, a special ornament of the town to this day, and originally the 'pleasance' to the Tudor palace turned to good account as a 'village green'; or sauntered along the riverside and contemplated the most famous view in England, a gift to the Claudian artist. Not surprisingly, men distinguished in the arts, especially in music, drama, literature and painting, resided at Richmond to be with their wealthy patrons. They included James Thomson, author of *The Seasons*, the most unqualified tribute to the Thames landscape, and the tragedian, Edmund Kean, both buried in the parish church. Others included Thomas Gainsborough, the artist, buried at Kew, David Garrick, Richard Sheridan and Sir Joshua Reynolds, the first president of the Royal Academy, whose country house on Richmond Hill was designed by the architect, Sir William Chambers, also the designer of the Pagoda, Orangery and temples erected in the royal grounds of the White House, Kew, still existing in the present Royal Botanical Gardens. The painting entitled 'Richmond Hill on the Prince Regent's birthday, 1819', by J.M.W. Turner, R.A. (himself a local resident) is probably the best visible expression of the gaiety and brilliance of the affluent society that gathered on the banks of the river Thames in the manner of the gay folk in one of Watteau's pictures.

The **Royal Borough of Kingston-upon-Thames** has been robbed of its physical identity and economic prosperity as a market town by London's sprawl. Victorians, fearful of Kingston's future, gloried in its great past, notably as the place of coronation of Saxon kings of Wessex. W.D. Biden observed in 1852 that the stone on which monarchs sat during the coronation ceremony had been preserved 'with almost religious veneration'. It was re-sited in a prominent position near the market place in 1850. Medieval Kingston was a clothing town. In the 17th century knitwear was added and

malting and tanning continued to be important. It also functioned as an important local market, and as an assize town it had the responsibility of making judges comfortable. Although Kingston prepared itself for a modern rôle by building a new bridge across the Thames to replace its wooden one in 1828 and constructing a Town Hall (now the Market House) in 1838, the main event of the 19th century was the development of the New Town on Surbiton Hill which lay on the line of the South-Western Railway. Biden noted sadly, 'There are no places of public amusement or recreation in Kingston; and indeed the place is altogether more distinguished for what it was not than for what it has'. In fact Kingston revived in its new rôle as a major retailing centre for its area of Greater London, led by the family of Bentall.

Croydon is the supreme example of the transformation by urban expansion from a rural market town to an outer metropolitan 'dormitory suburb'. In the early 19th century its economic function was dual, that of a coaching town on the main highway to Brighton and as a market for agricultural produce. The heavy

110 Modern urban sprawl, Woking. This evoked the expression 'rurban' coined in 1931 for the kind of human settlement that was neither town nor country but a hybrid of the two, sprouting pseudo-Tudor 'cottages' more frequently than trees. It was a half-realisation of H.G. Wells' prediction in Anticipations *(1900) that '... the city will diffuse itself until it has taken up considerable areas ... The country will take to itself many of the qualities of the city ...'.*

passing traffic provided work for one quarter of its traders as innkeepers, blacksmiths, saddlers, harness makers and wheelwrights. Although in 1802 one of the earliest public railways was opened between Wandsworth and Croydon for horse-drawn vehicles and the Croydon Canal was constructed in 1809, '... the long narrow High Street stretched southward, dull rather than quiet, with here a slow grey-tilted carrier's cart, and there a Brighton stage-coach stopping to change horses. A little further on were the rest of the sleepy shops on the right and left, and over the way the local Capitol, where farmers stood on market days behind their samples of corn on the ground floor.' Prior to the Croydon Enclosure Act of 1797 one third of the parish of nearly 10,000 acres lay in commonalty as open and common fields and meadows, wastes, commonable woodland and commons.

Remorselessly, this once rural area was encroached upon by the urban conglomerate of South London. The period of greatest population growth was between 1851-91 and Croydon's population reached 170,000 in 1914.

Dr. Cox has shown that migration of working-class people from Surrey villages and of middle classes from London were responsible for the urbanisation of eight former hamlets in Croydon parish, such as Thornton Heath, Norbury, Upper and South Norwood. The 11 railway stations in the parish by 1870 indicate that Croydon's growth was more affected by railways than most centres. Croydon was the worst damaged of south London boroughs during the Second World War.

Croydon now has a population of over 250,000 people and since the 1960s has created some of the most advanced planning and architecture in Britain, the result of the move of commercial firms from inner London. The once famous aerodrome is now an industrial and residential estate.

The origin of **Woking** is the strangest of the Surrey towns created in the Age of Steam. The railway station was sited in 1838 on a heath two miles from historic Old Woking with its parish church. In the 1850s the Necropolis Company bought 2,000 acres of land for the first and largest necropolis under the London Necropolis Act of 1852 which provided for the burial of London citizens beyond the confines of the metropolis to avoid the risk of cholera. Thus Surrey began to provide space not only for London's living but also for its dead, conveyed 25 miles by steam train to their final resting place at Brookwood cemetery, once served by a branch line with two little wooden stations (one for Anglicans, one for Nonconformists, Catholics and Parsees). Brookwood was also chosen as the location of public institutions created by various reforming Acts of Parliament, such as a lunatic asylum in 1867 and a women's prison (later converted into barracks). A crematorium was constructed in 1878 in the St John's district and in 1889 Dr Gottlieb Leitner built the onion-domed Shah Jehan mosque in Oriental Road near the centre for the Oriental and Islamic studies he had founded earlier.

What had been a parish of 1,975 in 1831 became a town of 36,000 in 1931 and with the electrification of the railway commuters steadily increased. In post-war years a massive relocation of offices from London and its resultant modern urban sprawl makes it the epitome of the general urge of professional, managerial and white-collar workers to flock to once-green countryside.

In locomotion, the Surrey railways were fast superseding road traffic in mid-Victorian times. Steam was first used for crossing the Weald in 1841, when the London to Brighton railway opened. **Redhill** sprang up around a railway station on this line and with the construction of branch lines to Reading and Ashford speculative land companies so successfully 'boomed' its railway advantages that the modern town of Redhill had by 1861 outstripped in population its mother town of Reigate, a typical decaying coaching town. In few Surrey places is the juxtaposition of the Victorian and earlier ages, and the differing social, political, architectural and economic values they embodied, so vividly contrasted as in this once single parish. It was also a symptom of the too rapidly urbanising environment which has since dislocated Surrey.

19

The Austere Present: Surrey since 1939

> There's no space. I never saw a more spreading lot of animals in my life, all in the wrong places.
>
> A.A. Milne, *The House at Pooh Corner*

Within minutes of the declaration of war on 3 September 1939 the wail of air raid sirens symbolised that Surrey, again part of the 'cornerstone of England', was on front-line alert. Yet not until the Germans occupied France and the Low Countries in May 1940 did they secure the necessary bases to attempt to force the Channel. This led to the famous Battle of Britain over Kent, Surrey and Sussex in August and September 1940 which saved Britain from Nazi occupation, owing to the resistance of Royal Air Force pilots operating against the Luftwaffe from airfields at Kenley, Biggin Hill, Hornchurch and Tangmere.

Raymond Chudley's diary records epic moments in the battle of the sky above Guildford:

> Monday 9 September 1940, 5.45-6.30pm
> 55 Junkers 88 [bombers] in box formation. Spitfires seen victory rolling.
>
> Monday 30 September. Terrific dogfight over Onslow Village. Machine gun fire like a violent storm.

In the concluding stage of the war, Surrey became a crucial springboard for the seaborne allied assault upon Europe in June 1944. Country houses and their estates were commandeered for Canadian troops; remote rural areas were supplied for the first time with piped water and electricity; new roads were constructed by the Canadians, including part of the Leatherhead bypass and many by-ways were metalled. In the months up to D-Day and up to the end of the war thousands of army vehicles, mostly amphibious 'ducks', were stored under camouflage in holding bays and repair yards, as on the carriageway of the A24 in the Vale of Mickleham. Extensive areas of Surrey heaths near Aldershot were used as military training grounds and large parts of the North Downs were sealed off to the public. Headley Heath was in a deplorable state when the war finished, churned up by military vehicles, its heather and trees largely destroyed. Much pasture on the Downs and in the Weald was brought under the plough for the first time for up to fifty years.

James Chuter-Ede's diary is an indispensable source of information about Surrey at war. Although a government minister, he travelled everywhere by bus like everyone else and queued patiently at shops for the minuscule rations and special treats: 'Monday 8 February 1943 ... I called at the United Dairies [in Epsom] to try to put our name down for some sausages. The girl told me the list was full for the 13th and 20th so I told her to put us down for the 27th'.

From mid-1944 until the end of the war Surrey, with the rest of London and the South East, came under heavy aerial bombardment, this time from unmanned missiles ('doodle-

bugs' or 'flying bombs') launched from the French and Dutch coasts and, later, from rockets (V2s). Over 3,000 flying bombs rained on London and its suburbs in five weeks. Parts of Surrey, with Sussex and Kent, became known as 'bomb alley' because they lay along the route of flying bombs falling short of their target of London.

111 Enlightened estate housing, Shere, by Reginald Bray (d.1950). Bray took exceptional interest in housing farm workers and valiantly strove to keep enough 'foreigners' away to keep cottages affordable.

Paradise Lost

During the post-war era, Surrey has changed more rapidly and radically and with greater consequences than ever before. This has put the absorp-

tive and adaptive tradition of the county to its severest test. With the decline of the industrial North and Midlands, the South East has been Britain's most economically advanced and successful region (but by the standards of a declining world-power economically). Surrey's overwhelmingly middle-class white-collar workers are wealthier, healthier, better educated and earning more Gross Domestic Product per head than those elsewhere in the country, but Surrey's high achievers pay a high price for this in stress of commuting and long working hours which are said to account for the high divorce rate, the highest in Europe.

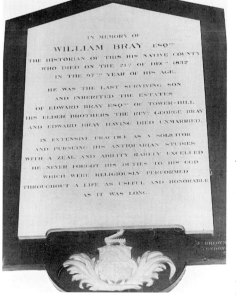

112 A monument in Shere church to William Bray, the famous Surrey historian and the first editor of John Evelyn's Diaries. His descendant, Reginald Bray (d.1950) was a pioneer conservationist who, between the two World Wars, was instrumental, with the help of others, in saving from the builder the Leith Hill district and large tracts of the North Downs. He was actively supported by James Chuter Ede, as chairman of Surrey County Council, and the County earned credit for a vigorous campaign to protect for posterity key vulnerable parts of the countryside.

113 Interior of Gatton Church near Reigate furnished by Lord Monson in the 1840s with medieval and 16th-century 'cast offs' from continental religious institutions.

Since the 1960s, the energetic policy of planning the movement of people out of the capital into the suburbs and beyond to medium and small-sized towns, together with a general urge of the more affluent to move out into green countryside, has resulted in professional, managerial and white-collar workers flocking out of London into Surrey and the rest of the South East. The expansion of places such as Frimley, Woking and Guildford arose from this need to assist the escape from London, but now in their enlarged form they are themselves creating in their turn a new need to escape. Some Surrey towns now have an urban fringe degraded and run-down and fore-runners of the modern fashionable suburb such as Richmond and Epsom, and innumerable once traditional villages like Malden and the Dittons have lost nearly all their old identity, and having lost it, underwent an orgy of post-war development. The once-proud Kingston-upon-Thames, deriving its name from early Saxon under-kings of Surrey and where later West Saxon kings were crowned, is an instance. Ian Nairn wrote: 'What little there is of serious interest in the centre can rarely be seen for buses, cars and lorries'.

It has now become recognised that the once-bouyant economic opportunities of Surrey and the quality of its life-style are being more and more qualified by congestion and pollution. Those clogged up on the M25 or

114 The mansion named Reigate Priory, on the site of Reigate Priory, founded by the 6th Earl William Warenne c.1235, became the home of Lord William Howard of Effingham, Lord High Admiral at the time of the Spanish Armada. In the Edwardian era it was let to such personalities as Lord Curzon and the Hon. Mrs. Ronald Greville, who often entertained King Edward VII, leading politicians, poets and writers at glamorous parties. Eventually bought by Reigate Council, the house and grounds are a splendid part of Reigate's heritage.

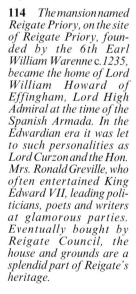

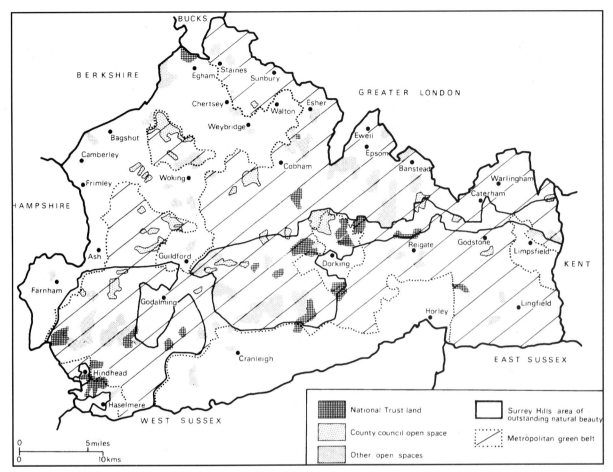

115 *Surrey: successive post-war increase in protection for the countryside.*

potentially affected by growth at Heathrow and Gatwick airports have been amongst the first to join in a strong backlash against the development nostrums of the 1960s. The most remarkable examples have concerned road traffic. In 1991 the Surrey County Council became the first authority in Britain far-sighted enough to recognise that it could not meet in full the future demand for road transport. In 1995 the banding together of the Council with the Surrey Society (affiliated to the Council for the Protection of Rural England), the National Trust and other organisations, defeated the government proposal to widen the M25 in Surrey between the M3 and M4 to 14 lanes. Recent years have also seen the rise of strong anti-populationist views against further growth and its consequences.

Although some of the bloom has gone from the Surrey scene, it is still people's preference to live in a Barratt home in commuter countryside than in a flat in inner London. This social trend remains alarming for the future of Surrey. The perennial dream of a house in Surrey never seems to lose its hold. It is incredible what lengths people will go to, and what money they will be persuaded to part with, for the realisation of a dream of a Surrey house and garden.

116 *The former orangery at Bury Hill, near Dorking. The country house was initially built by Edward Walter in 1756 on a new site chosen for its magnificent views. The estate passed to the Barclays, the brewing family, whose model farmery and bailiff's cottage was illustrated and praised by J.C. Loudon in his* Encyclopedia of Cottage Farm and Villa Architecture *(1839). A fire destroyed the central portion of the house after the Second World War. A fine landscaped lake, together with many estate cottages and buildings, survives and the new angling lakes and tree planting have recently been undertaken.*

These pressures have placed Surrey in mortal danger of being swallowed up like Middlesex, but it has adapted itself, unevenly and often reluctantly, but, on the whole, not unsuccessfully, to these changes. That Surrey survived this, its greatest crisis, is largely due to the concept of the Metropolitan Green Belt, the primary barrier erected against the tumbling disorder of a metropolis on the move. This idea developed out of the voluntary preservation of Surrey's countryside before the Second World War. Successive outward designation of the Green Belt curbed the outward growth of London and saved Surrey from wholesale disfigurement as a vast commuter dormitory. Unhappily, the Belt includes a medley of land uses, many existing before designation of the Belt, producing a 'strange hermaphrodite sort of landscape, half country, half town, of extremely doubtful value to Londoners or anyone else'.

Although Surrey is generally imagined as a costly and prosperous 'Yuppie' idyll, its old borders contain an extraordinary set of contrasts in living conditions, at once glamorous and squalid, seductive and repellent, successful and serene. A 'Domesday 1998' would disclose at one extreme the ghettoised society of inner south London with no jobs or prospects where the whole base of semi-skilled and unskilled manual work collapsed with the closure of the Port of London and the mass of factories and workshops which still existed as recently as 1977, the date of the first edition of this history. Yet the tide is turning for the old Surrey riverside with the prospect of the

Jubilee line opening to Canada Wharf in 1998 and house-buyers and developers are returning again. Moreover, when the world's camera was first focused on Brixton this run-down south London suburb was still shaken by riot, exacerbated by racial tensions. Then again, on the occasion of President Mandela's visit in 1996, the cameras were there to record a burst of civic and ethnic pride which has lasting lessons for England.

At the other extreme is the 'Stockbroker', 'Cocktail' or 'Sun' Belt of Surrey, 'a land of large drives and even larger houses. The land of cocktails and G and Ts' which Julian Critchley remarks has become 'chi chi, as bogus as such Surrey towns as Farnham where the front doors are all painted a pastel pink and even the policemen talk posh'. Between these two extremes less than arcadian reaches abound, such as the Blackwater valley on the western edge of the county which is currently being enhanced, and a remarkable diversity exists even between neighbouring settlements. Sheila Mackay, for example, has recently described Reigate as a 'genteel world of bijou cottages, kept gardens and bedizened ladies discreetly buying gin at Cullens' whereas Redhill was represented a decade ago as 'in essence a car park, or series of car parks, strung out together with links of smouldering rubble and ragwort, buddleia and willowherb'.

The challenge today is how to manage the massive rise of motor-car use, without slicing to ribbons and concreting what remains of Surrey's still breath-taking mix of 'wildness' and soft, tamed beauty. Surrey has become a test case as to whether its society is prepared to protect—or allow to be suburbanised and so irretrievably lost—further tracts of countryside. Another

117 Polesden Lacey in its earlier state was lived in by Richard Brinsley Sheridan who described it as 'The nicest place, within a prudent distance of town, in England'. It was rebuilt as a Grecian villa in 1824 with more concern for atmosphere than for accuracy, and was greatly extended in 1906 when the interior became Edwardian. Mrs. Ronald Greville evoked sumptuous mock Louis XIV with wall mirrors, ornate pilasters, imported French Rococco fireplaces and Italian ceiling paintings in the manner of Apsley House, Osterley, Goodwood and Windsor Castle in the Regency. It is now greatly valued as one of the last expressions of the style in the last few years before the First World War.

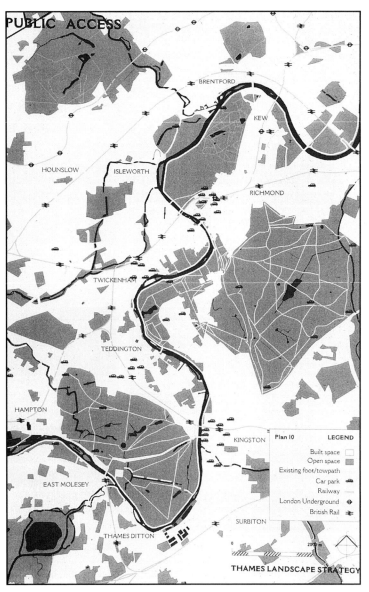

118 *The Thames Landscape Strategy proposed by Kim Wilkie and his associates in 1994 envisages integrated policies, projects and landscape management for the entire stretch of the riverside between Hampton Court and Kew. The object is to ensure that this legacy of the past is managed for the future.*

worrying trend is the decline in farming, with a corresponding increase in golf courses and 'horsey-culture'. The loss of such habitats as downland, woodland and heath is rightly regarded as a catastrophe, yet as H.E. Bates was first to observe with the loss of the farmland scene we should be faced with a still deeper catastrophe, 'the loss of a kind of beauty which we take as naturally for granted as the air we breathe'.

Surrey still occupies a special place in the heart of the nation. The survival of its beauty, as we have noted, is not the result of accident but to constant vigilance and energetic action of landowners, farmers and planners and public-spirited individuals and voluntary bodies. It is largely to those who have sweated and toiled, cajoled and implored, pleaded and beseeched, led deputations to ministers, waylaid M.P.s, written letters to *The Times*, lobbied councillors and planning officers and, in sheer desperation, employed counsel, climbed trees or threatened to lie down in front of a bulldozer, that loved Surrey owes its precarious survival today and it is only by similar exertions that it will be saved for the future.

Bibliography

The publications of the Surrey Archaeological Society (founded in 1854) comprise more than 80 volumes of the *Collections*, and a number of important Research Papers (two series). The Surrey Record Society has published over 30 volumes of transcribed documents. An extensive use of these publications has been made in this *History* which it is not possible to list here.

The main collections of original documents relating to Surrey are deposited in the Surrey County Council Record Offices at Kingston and Guildford, the Local History Library, Guildford and also at the Minet Library, Brixton. The Libraries of the London Boroughs of Richmond-upon-Thames, Southwark and Wimbledon, amongst others, have important collections of source material. The muniments of Merton College, Oxford relating to its medieval Surrey manors of Chessington, Farleigh, Leatherhead and Old Malden are important. These collections have been considerably drawn upon for this *History*. The main class of documents utilised in the Public Record Office, Chancery Lane, has been the *Inquisitiones Post Mortem* (1272-1340). As the citation of references in the text is impracticable in this book the main original sources used are indicated, by subject, at the end of this Bibliography. Of the landscape artists and water colourists mentioned, John Linnell is represented by collections at the Tate Gallery, and the Museum of London and also at the Bury, Preston and City of Birmingham and Manchester Galleries; the largest collection of Samuel Palmer's works is at the Ashmolean Museum, Oxford; J.M.W. Turner's sketchbooks are in the Department of Prints and Drawings of the British Library. The Fitzwilliam Museum, Cambridge, contains important 17th-century paintings of Richmond-upon-Thames.

(N.B. Books cited in the text are not included in the Bibliography.)

Aubrey, John, *The Natural History and Antiquities of the County of Surrey* (1718-19, reprinted 1975)
Bassett, Steven (ed.), *The Origins of Anglo-Saxon Kingdoms* (1989)
Batey, Mavis, *et al.*, *Arcadian Thames* (1995)
Batey, Mavis, *et al.*, *Jane Austen and the English Landscape* (1996)
Bird, Joanna and D.G., *The Archaeology of Surrey to 1540* (1987)
Bird, Margaret, *Holmbury St. Mary: One Hundred Years* (1979)
Blair, John, *Early Medieval Surrey* (1991)
Blatch, Mervyn, *The Churches of Surrey* (1997)
Blomfield, Reginald, *Richard Norman Shaw, R.A.* (1940)
Brandon, Peter and Short, Brian, *The South East from A.D. 1000* (1990)
Brayley, E.W., *History of Surrey* (5 vols., 1850)
British Association, *The Surrey Countryside* (1975)
Brown, Jane, *Gardens of a Golden Afternoon* (1982)
Brown, Jane, *Lutyens and the Edwardians* (1996)
Brown, Richard, *Domestic Architecture* (1841)
Caird, James, *English Agriculture in 1850-1* (1852, 1968)
Chamberlin, E.R., *Biography of Guildford* (1970)
Clayton-Payne, Andrew, *Victorian Cottages* (1993)

Cline, C.L. (ed.), *The Letters of George Meredith* (1970)

Cloake, John, *The Palaces and Parks of Richmond and Kew* (2 vols., 1995/6)

Cobbett, William, *Rural Rides* (ed. G.D.H. and Margaret Cole, 1930)

Connell, John H., *The End of Tradition: Country Life in Central Surrey* (1978)

Cooper, Phyllis M., *The Story of Claremont* (1983)

Cornish, Charles, *Wild England Today* (1900)

Courlander, K., *Richmond* (1953)

Cracknell, Basil E., *Portrait of Surrey* (1974)

Crocker, Alan, *Paper Mills of the Tillingbourne: a history of paper making in a Surrey valley 1704 to 1875* (1988)

Darby, H.C. and Campbell, E.M.J., *The Domesday Geography of South-East England* (1971)

Defoe, Daniel, *A Tour Through Great Britain* (1738)

Drewett, P., Rudling, D. and Gardiner, M., *The South East to A.D. 1000* (1988)

Evison, V.I., *The Fifth-Century Invasions South of the Thames* (1965)

Forge, L.W. Lindus and Collier, Mavis, *Painshill* (1986)

Gibbs, Sir Philip, *England Speaks* (sections IV and V contain much on Surrey between the wars)

Gover, J.E.B., Mawer, A. and Stenton, F.M., *The Place-Names of Surrey*, English Place Name Society, vol.XI (1934)

Gradidge, Roderick, *Dream Houses: The Edwardian Ideal* (1980)

Gradidge, Roderick, *The Surrey Style* (1991)

Gray, H.L., *English Field Systems* (1915)

Gray, Peter, *Bletchingly: Village and Parish* (1991)

Gray, Peter, *Charlwood Houses* (1978)

Green, Candida Lycett (ed.), *John Betjeman: Letters* (2 vols., 1994-5)

Haight, Gordon, S., *The George Eliot Letters* (1954-5)

Hall, A.D. and Russell, E.J., *Agriculture and Soils of Kent, Surrey and Sussex* (1911)

Hayward Gallery, *Lutyens* (1981)

Hooper, Wilfrid, *Reigate: Its Story through the Ages* (1945)

Hoskins, W.G., *The Making of the English Landscape* (1988, 1992)

Huish, M.B., *Happy England as Painted by Mrs. Allingham* (1982)

Huish, M.B., *Birket Foster* (1980)

Hussey, Christopher, *English Gardens and Landscapes, 1700-1750* (1967)

Hutchings, G.E., *The Book of Box Hill* (1952)

Janaway, John, *Surrey: A County History* (1994)

Jekyll, Francis, *Gertrude Jekyll* (1934)

Jekyll, Gertrude, *Wood and Garden* (1899)

Jessup, R.F., *The Archaeology of South-East England* (1970)

Jones, Pamela Fletcher, *Richmond Park* (1983)

Kenyon, G. Hugh, *The Wealden Glass Industry* (1967)

Longworth, Ian and Cherry, John, *Archaeology in Britain since 1945* (1986)

Loudon, James, *An Encyclopaedia of Gardening* (1826)

Loudon, James, *Cottage Farm and Villa Architecture* (1857)

Loudon, James, *Country Residences* (1858)

Mack, M., *The Garden and the City* (1969)

Malcolm, James, *A Compendium of Modern Husbandry* (1805)

Manning, Elfrida, *Saxon Farnham* (1970)

Margary, I.D., *Roman Ways in the Weald* (1948)

Marsh, Anne, *Heathside Farm* (1863) (a novel set in West Surrey)

Marshall, W., *The Economy of the Southern Counties* (1798)

Mason, R.T., *Framed Buildings of the Weald* (1964)

Massingham, Betty, *Miss Jekyll: A Portrait of a Great Gardener* (1966)

Morris, John R., *The Age of Arthur* (1973)

Nairn, Ian and Pevsner, Nikolaus, *The Buildings of England: Surrey* (2nd ed., 1971)

Ogden, Margaret and H.V.S., *English Taste in Landscape in the Seventeenth Century* (1935)

Parker, Eric, *Highways and Byways in Surrey* (1909)

Pollard, E., Hooper, M.D. and Moore, N.W., *Hedges* (1974)

Rankine, W.F., *The Mesolithic of South England* (1956)

Reynolds, Peter J., *Farming in the Iron Age* (1976)

Robinson, William, *The Wild Garden* (1870)

Shere, Gomshall and Peaslake Local History Society, *Old Houses in the Parish of Shere* (1981)

Smith, Eric E.F., *Clapham* (1976)

Stamp, Gavin and Goulancourt, André, *The English House 1860-1914* (1986)

Straker, E., *Wealden Iron* (1931)

Stroud, D., *Capability Brown* (1954)

Stroud, D., *Humphry Repton* (1962)

Surrey Garden Trust, *Art and Crafts Architecture and Gardens in and around Guildford* (1993)

Switzer, S., *Ichnographia Rustica* (1742)

Symes, Michael, *William Gilpin at Painshill* (1994)

Temple, N., *Farnham Buildings and People* (1972)

Trotter, W.R., *The Hilltop Writers: A Writers' Colony in Surrey* (1996)

Vardey, Edwina, *History of Leatherhead* (1988)

Victoria and Albert Museum, *Richard Redgrave* (1988)

Vulliamy, C.E., *The Onslow Family, 1528-1874* (1953)

Warren, John (ed.), *Wealden Buildings* (1990)

Wells, H.G., *Mr. Britling Sees it Through* (1916)

Wells, H.G., *The History of Mr. Polly* (1910)

White, Gilbert, *The Natural History and Antiquities of Selborne* (1826)

Williams-Ellis, Clough, *Architect Errant* (1971)

Wilson, J.B., *The Story of Norwood* (1973)

Wooldridge, S.W. and Goldring, F., *The Weald* (1953)

References to Original Sources

Christ Church College, Oxford: Evelyn Papers (for material in Chapter 11) (The MS. is now in the British Library)

Guildford Muniment Room: Loseley Mss. 637, 729, 757, 955/1/2, 154/1-42 (Guildford cloth-making); Reginald Bray papers

Surrey County Record Office, Kingston: 329/13/1-4, 14/1-2 (18th-century agriculture)

Minet Library, Brixton: Collection of drawings and prints and documents 592 (Lambeth), 1574 (Camberwell), 2846-50, 2854, 6, 8 (Portnall, Egham), 3606 (medieval hunting), 3618 (Tandridge Priory), 3764 (Merton weaving)

Public Record Office, London: *Inquisitiones Post Mortem*; Ministers Accounts, Surrey; Forest Account, Surrey; Hearth Tax returns

Victoria and Albert Museum Mss: H.34 (Thames-side landscape)

British Library: interleaved copy of Manning and Bray, *History and Antiquities of Surrey* (1847), 30 vols.

Wimbledon Reference Library: interleaved Brayley, *History of Surrey* (5 vols.)

Index

Numbers in **bold** type indicate page numbers of illustrations in the text.
Roman numerals indicate colour plates.